IN THE SCHOOL-ROOM.

CHAPTERS IN THE PHILOSOPHY OF EDUCATION.

JOHN S. HART, LL. D.,
PRINCIPAL OF THE NEW JERSEY STATE NORMAL SCHOOL.

PHILADELPHIA:
ELDREDGE & BROTHER,
17 AND 19 SOUTH SIXTH STREET.
1868.

J. FAGAN & SON,
STEREOTYPE FOUNDERS,
PHILADELPHIA.

PRINTED BY SHERMAN & CO.

TO THE

Teachers of the United States,

AND ESPECIALLY TO THE

ALUMNI OF THE PHILADELPHIA HIGH SCHOOL,

AND OF THE

New Jersey State Normal School,

THE FOLLOWING CHAPTERS

ARE

MOST RESPECTFULLY DEDICATED

BY THE AUTHOR.

PREFACE.

THE views contained in this volume are the result of a prolonged and somewhat varied professional experience. This experience includes the training of more than five thousand young men and of nearly one thousand young women, a large portion of them for the office of teachers; and it has been gained in College, in Boarding School, in a city High School, and in a State Normal School. In all this prolonged and varied experience, I have constantly put myself in the attitude of a learner, and my aim in the present volume is to place before the younger members of the profession, in the briefest and clearest terms possible, the lessons I have myself learned. Beginning with the question, What is Teaching? and ending with the wider question, What is Education? the book will be found to take a pretty free range over the whole field of practical inquiry among professional teachers. The thoughts presented are such as have been suggested to the writer in the school-room itself, while actively engaged either in teaching, or in superintending and directing the instruction given by others. These thoughts are for the most part purposely given in short, detached chapters, each complete in itself. Such a method of presentation, though less imposing, seemed to have practical advantages for the reader too great to be neglected for the mere vanity of authorship. Often one can find leisure to read a chapter of five or six pages on some point complete in itself, when he might not feel like reaching it through an intervening network of connected and dependent propositions. At the same time, it should be observed, the topics though detached are not isolated. There is everywhere an underlying thread of connection, the whole being based upon, if not constituting, a philosophy of education.

CONTENTS.

IN THE SCHOOL-ROOM.

I.

WHAT IS TEACHING?

IN the first place, teaching is not simply telling. A class may be told a thing twenty times over, and yet not know it. Talking to a class is not necessarily teaching. I have known many teachers who were brimful of information, and were good talkers, and who discoursed to their classes with ready utterance a large part of the time allotted to instruction; yet an examination of their classes showed little advancement in knowledge.

There are several time-honored metaphors on this subject, which need to be received with some grains of allowance, if we would get at an exact idea of what teaching is. Chiselling the rude marble into the finished statue; giving the impression of the seal upon the soft wax; pouring water into an empty vessel;—all these comparisons lack one essential element of likeness. The mind is, indeed, in one sense, empty, and needs to be filled. It is yielding, and needs to be impressed. It is rude, and needs polishing. But it is not, like the marble, the wax, or the vessel, a passive recipient of external influences. It is itself a living power. It is acted upon only by stirring up its own activities. The operative upon mind, unlike the operative upon matter, must have the active, voluntary co-operation of that upon which he works. The teacher is doing his work, only so far as he gets work from the scholar. The very essence and root of the work are in the scholar, not in the teacher. No one, in fact, in an important sense, is taught at all, except so far as he is self-taught. The teacher may be useful, as an auxiliary, in causing this action on the part of the scholar. But the one, indispensable, vital thing in all learning, is in the scholar himself. The old Romans, in their word education (*educere*, to draw out), seem to have come nearer to the true idea than any other people have done. The teacher is to draw out the resources of the pupil. Yet even this word comes short of the exact truth. The teacher must put in, as well as draw out. No process of mere pumping will draw out from a child's mind knowledge which is not there. All the power of the Socratic method, could it be applied by Socrates himself, would be unavailing to draw from a child's mind, by mere questioning, a knowledge, for instance, of chemical affinity, of the solar system, of the temperature of the Gulf Stream, of the doctrine of the resurrection.

What, then, is teaching?

Teaching is causing any one to know. Now no one can be made to know a thing but by the act of his own powers. His own senses, his own memory, his own powers of reason, perception, and judgment, must be exercised. The function of the teacher is to bring about this exercise of the pupil's faculties. The means to do this are infinite in variety. They should be varied according to the wants and the character of the individual to be taught. One needs to be told a thing; he learns most readily by the ear. Another needs to use his eyes; he must see a thing, either in the book, or in nature. But neither eye nor ear, nor any other sense or faculty, will avail to the acquisition of knowledge, unless the power of attention is cultivated. Attention, then, is the first act or power of the mind that must be roused. It is the very foundation of all progress in knowledge, and the means of awakening it constitute the first step in the educational art.

When by any means, positive knowledge, facts, are once in possession of the mind, something must next be done to prevent their slipping away. You may tell a class the history of a certain event; or you may give them a description of a certain place or person; or you may let them read it; and you may secure such a degree of attention, that, at the time of the reading or the description, they shall have a fair, intelligible comprehension of what has been described or read. The facts are for the time actually in the possession of the mind. Now, if the mind was, according to the old notion, merely a vessel to be filled, the process would be complete. But mind is not an empty vessel. It is a living essence, with powers and processes of its own. And experience shows us, that in the case of a class of undisciplined pupils, facts, even when fairly placed in the possession of the mind, often remain there about as long as the shadow of a passing cloud remains upon the landscape, and make about as much impression.

The teacher must seek, then, not only to get knowledge into the mind, but to fix it there. In other words, the power of the memory must be strengthened. Teaching, then, most truly, and in every stage of it, is a strictly co-operative process. You cannot cause any one to know, by merely pouring out stores of knowledge in his hearing, any more than you can make his body grow by spreading the contents of your market-basket at his feet. You must rouse his power of attention, that he may lay hold of, and receive, and make his own, the knowledge you offer him. You must awaken and strengthen the power of memory within him, that he may retain what he receives, and thus grow in knowledge, as the body by a like process grows in strength and muscle. In other words, learning, so far as the mind of the learner is concerned, is a growth; and teaching, so far as the teacher is concerned, is doing whatever is necessary to cause that growth.

Let us proceed a step farther in this matter.

One of the ancients observes that a lamp loses none of its own light by allowing another lamp to be lit from it. He uses the illustration to enforce the duty of liberality in imparting our knowledge to others. Knowledge, he says, unlike other treasures, is not diminished by giving.

The illustration fails to express the whole truth. This imparting of knowledge to others, not only does not impoverish the donor, but it actually increases his riches. *Docendo discimus.* By teaching we learn. A man grows in knowledge by the very act of communicating it. The reason for this is obvious. In order to communicate to the mind of another a thought which is in our own mind, we must give to the thought definite shape and form. We must handle it, and pack it up for safe conveyance. Thus the mere act of giving a thought expression in words, fixes it more deeply in our own minds. Not only so; we can, in fact, very rarely be said to be in full possession of a thought ourselves, until by the tongue or the pen we have communicated it to somebody else. The expression of it, in some form, seems necessary to give it, even in our own minds, a definite shape and a lasting impression. A man who devotes himself to solitary reading and study, but never tries in any way to communicate his acquisitions to the world, or to enforce his opinions upon others, rarely becomes a learned man. A great many confused, dreamy ideas, no doubt, float through the brain of such a man; but he has little exact and reliable knowledge. The truth is, there is a sort of indolent, listless absorption of intellectual food, that tends to idiocy. I knew a person once, a gentleman of wealth and leisure, who having no taste for social intercourse, and no material wants to be supplied, which might have required the active exercise of his powers, gave himself up entirely to solitary reading, as a sort of luxurious self-indulgence. He shut himself up in his room, all day long, day after day, devouring one book after another, until he became almost idiotic by the process, and he finally died of softening of the brain. Had he been compelled to use his mental acquisitions in earning his bread, or had the love of Christ constrained him to use them in the instruction of the poor and the ignorant, he might have become not only a useful, but a learned man.

We see a beautiful illustration of this doctrine in the case of Sabbath-school teachers, and one reason why persons so engaged usually love their work, is the benefit which they find in it for themselves. I speak here, not of the spiritual, but of the intellectual benefit. By the process of teaching others, they are all the while learning. This advantage in their case is all the greater, because it advances them in a kind of knowledge in which, more than in any other kind of knowledge, men are wont to become passive and stationary. In ordinary worldly knowledge, our necessities make us active. The intercourse of business, and of pleasure even, makes men keen. On these subjects we are all the while bandying thoughts to and fro; we are accustomed to give as well as take; and so we keep our intellectual armor bright, and our thoughts well defined. But in regard to growth in religious knowledge, we have a tendency to be mere passive recipients, like the young man just referred to. Sabbath after Sabbath we hear good, instructive, orthodox discourses, but there is no active putting forth of our own powers in giving out what we thus take in, and so we never make it effectually our own. The absorbing process goes on, and yet we make no growth. The quiescent audience is a sort of exhausted receiver, into which the stream from the pulpit is perennially playing, but never making it full. Let a man go back and ask himself, What actual scriptural knowledge have I gained by the sermons of the last six months? What in fact do I retain in my mind, at this moment, of the sermons I heard only a month ago? So far as the hearing of sermons is concerned, the Sabbath-school teacher may perhaps be no better off than other hearers. But in regard to general growth in religious knowledge, he advances more rapidly than his fellow-worshippers, because the exigencies of his class compel him to a state of mind the very opposite of this passive recipiency. He is obliged to be all the while, not only learning, but putting his acquisitions into definite shape for use, and the very act of using these acquisitions in teaching a class, fixes them in his own mind, and makes them more surely his own.

I have used this instance of the Sabbath-school teacher because it enforces an important hint already given, as to the mode of teaching. Some teachers, especially in Sabbath-schools, seem to be ambitious to do a great deal of talking. The measure of their success, in their own eyes, is their ability to keep up a continued stream of talk for the greater part of the hour. This is of course better than the embarrassing silence sometimes seen, where neither teacher nor scholar has anything to say. But at the best, it is only the pouring into the exhausted receiver enacted over again. We can never be reminded too often, that there is no teaching except so far as there is active coöperation on the part of the learner. The mind receiving must reproduce and give back what it gets. This is the indispensable condition of making any knowledge really our own. The very best teaching I have ever seen, has been where the teacher said comparatively little. The teacher was of course brimful of the subject. He could give the needed information at exactly the right point, and in the right quantity. But for every word given by the teacher, there were many words of answering reproduction on the part of the scholars. Youthful minds under such tutelage grow apace.

It is indeed a high and difficult achievement in the educational art, to get young persons thus to bring forth their thoughts freely for examination and correction. A pleasant countenance and a gentle manner, inviting and inspiring confidence, have something to do with the matter. But, whatever the means for accomplishing this end, the end itself is indispensable. The scholar's tongue must be unloosed, as well as the teacher's. The scholar's thoughts must be broached, as well as the teacher's. Indeed, the statement needs very little qualification or abatement, that a scholar has learned nothing from us except what he has expressed to us again in words. The teacher who is accustomed to harangue his scholars with a continuous stream of words, no matter how full of weighty meaning his words may be, is yet deceiving himself, if he thinks that his scholars are materially benefited by his intellectual activity, unless it is so guided as to awaken and exercise theirs. If, after a suitable period, he will honestly examine his scholars on the subjects, on which he has himself been so productive, he will find that he has been only pouring water into a sieve. Teaching can never be this one-sided process. Of all the things we attempt, it is the one most essentially and necessarily a coöperative process. There must be the joint action of the teacher's mind and the scholar's mind. A teacher teaches at all, only so far as he causes this coactive energy of the pupil's mind.

II.

THE ART OF QUESTIONING.

THE measure of a teacher's success is not what he himself does, but what he gets his scholars to do. In nothing is this more noticeable, than in the different modes of putting a question to a scholar. One teacher will put a question in such a manner as to find out exactly how much or how little of the subject the child knows, and thereby encourage careful preparation; to give the pupil an open door, if he really knows the subject, to express his knowledge in a way that will be a satisfaction and pleasure to him; to improve his power of expression, to cultivate his memory, to increase his knowledge, and to make it more thorough and definite. Another teacher will put his questions so as to secure none of these ends, but on the contrary so as to induce a most lamentable degree of carelessness and inaccuracy.

Let me illustrate this point, taking an example for greater convenience from a scriptural subject. Suppose it to be a lesson upon Christ's temptation, as recorded in the 4th chapter of Matthew. The dialogue between teacher and scholar may be supposed to proceed somewhat in this wise:

Teacher. Who was led up of the Spirit into the wilderness to be tempted of the devil?

Pupil. Jesus.

T. Yes. Now, when Jesus had fasted forty days and

forty nights, he was afterward a—— what? How did he feel after that?

P. Hungry.

T. Yes, that is right. He was afterward "a hungered." Now, then, the next scholar. Who then came to Jesus and said, If thou be the Son of God, command that these stones be made bread?

(Scholar hesitates.)

T. The t——?

P. The tempter.

T. Yes, you are right. It was the tempter. Who do you think is meant by the tempter?—the devil?

P. Yes.

T. When a man has fasted, that is, has eaten nothing, for forty days and forty nights, and feels very hungry, would the suggestion of an easy mode of getting food be likely to be a strong temptation to him, or would it not?

P. It would.

T. Yes, you are right again. It would be a strong temptation to him.

I need not pursue this dialogue further. The reader will see at once how there may thus be the appearance of quite a brisk and fluent recitation, to which however the pupil contributes absolutely nothing. It requires nothing of him in the way of preparation, and only the most indolent and profitless use of his faculties while reciting. He could hardly answer amiss, unless he were an idiot, and yet he has the appearance, and he is often flattered into the belief, of having given some evidence of knowledge and proficiency.

The opposite extreme from the method just exhibited, is that known as the topical method. It is the method pursued in the higher classes of schools, and among more advanced students. In the topical method, the teacher propounds a topic or subject, sometimes in the form of a question, but more commonly only by a title, a mere word or two, and then calls upon the pupil to give, in his own words, a full and connected narration or explanation of the subject, such as the teacher himself would give, if called upon to narrate or explain it. The subject already suggested, if profound topically, would be somewhat in this wise:

The first temptation of Jesus.

Or, more fully: Narrate the circumstances of the first temptation of Jesus, and show wherein his virtue was particularly tried in that transaction.

The teacher, having propounded the subject clearly to the class, then waits patiently, maintaining silence himself, and requiring the members of the class to be silent and attentive, until the pupil interrogated is quite through, not hurrying him, not interrupting him, even with miscalled helps and hints, but leaving him to the free and independent action of his own faculties, in giving as full, connected, and complete an account of the matter as he can. When the pupil is quite through, the teacher then, but not before, makes any corrections or additional statements that may seem to be needed. In such an exercise as this, the pupil finds the absolute necessity of full and ample preparation; he has a powerful and healthy stimulus thus to prepare, in the intellectual satisfaction which one always feels in the successful discharge of any difficult task; and he acquires a habit of giving complete and accurate expression to his knowledge, by means of entire sentences, and without the help of "catch-words," or leading-strings of any kind.

Some classes, of course, are not sufficiently advanced to carry out fully the method here explained. But there are many intermediate methods, founded on the same principle, and suited to children in every stage of advancement. Only let it be understood, whatever the stage, that the object of the recitation is, not to show what the teacher can say or do, but to secure the right thing being said and done by the pupil.

To recur once more to the same subject, the temptation of Christ. For a very juvenile class, the questioning might proceed on this wise:

T. Where was Jesus led after his baptism?

P. He was led into the wilderness.

T. By whom was he led there?

P. He was led by the Spirit.

T. For what purpose was he led into the wilderness?

P. He was led into the wilderness to be tempted.

T. By whom was he to be tempted?

P. He was to be tempted by the devil.

T. What bodily want was made the means of his first temptation?

If the class is quite young, and this question seems too difficult, the teacher, instead of asking it, or after asking it and not getting a satisfactory answer, might say to his class, that Jesus was first tempted through the sense of hunger. He was very hungry, and the devil suggested to him an improper means of relieving himself from the inconvenience. He might then go on with some such questions as these:

T. What circumstance is mentioned as showing how very hungry he must have been?

P. He had fasted forty days and forty nights.

T. Mention any way in which *you* might be tempted to sin, if you were suffering from hunger?

The foregoing questions, it will be perceived, are very simple, being suited to scholars just advanced beyond the infant class. Yet no one of the questions, in its form, or terms, necessarily suggests the answer. No one of them can be answered by a mere "yes" or "no." No scholar, unacquainted with the subject, and with his book closed, can guess at the answer from the way in which the question is put. Not a question has been given, simple as they all are, which does not require some preparation, and which does not, to some extent, give exercise to the pupil's memory, his judgment, and his capacity for expression.

If the class is more advanced, the questions may be varied, so as to task and exercise these faculties more seriously. For instance, the teacher of a class somewhat older might be imagined to begin the exercise thus:

T. After the baptism of Jesus, which closes the 3d chapter of Matthew, we have an account of several temptations to which he was exposed. Now, open your books at the 4th chapter, and see if you can find out how many verses are occupied with the narrative of these temptations, and at what verse each temptation begins.

The teacher then requires all the class to search in silence, and each one to get ready to answer, but lets no answer be given until all are prepared. When all have signified their readiness, some one is designated to give the answer.

The books being closed, the questioning begins:

T. Name the different places into which Jesus was taken to be tempted, and the verse in which each place is named.

P. It is said in the 1st verse that Jesus was led up into the wilderness; in the 5th verse, that he was taken up into the holy city, and set on a pinnacle of the temple; and in the 8th verse, that he was taken up into an exceedingly high mountain.

T. What was the condition of Jesus, when the devil proposed his first temptation?

P. He had been fasting forty days and forty nights, and he was very hungry.

I need not multiply these illustrations. I have not made them entirely in vain, if I have succeeded in producing in the mind of the reader the conviction of these two things: first, that it is a most important and difficult part of the teacher's art, to know how to ask a question; and secondly, that the true measure of the teacher's ability is, not so much what he himself is able to say to the scholars, as the fulness, the accuracy, and the completeness of the answers which he gets from them.

III.

THE DIFFERENCE BETWEEN TEACHING AND TRAINING.

THESE two processes practically run into each other a good deal, but they ought not to be confounded. Training implies more or less of practical application of what one has been taught. One may be taught, for instance, the exact forms of the letters used in writing, so as to know at once by the eye whether the letters are formed correctly or not. But only training and practice will make him a penman. Training refers more to the formation of habits. A child may by reasoning be taught the importance of punctuality in coming to school; but he is trained to the habit of punctuality only by actually coming to school in good time, day after day.

The human machine on which the teacher acts, is in its essential nature different from the material agencies operated on by other engineers. It is, as I have once and again said, a living power, with laws and processes of its own. Constant care, therefore, must be exercised, in the business of education, not to be misled by analogies drawn from the material world. The steam-engine may go over its appointed task, day after day, the whole year round, and yet, at the end of the year, it will have no more tendency to go than before its first trip. Not so the boy. Going begets going. By doing a thing often, he acquires a facility, an inclination, a tendency, a habit of doing it. If a teacher or a parent succeeds in getting a child to do a thing once, it will be easier to get him to do it a second time, and still easier a third time.

A teacher who is wise, when he seeks to bring about any given change in a child, whether it be intellectual or moral, will not ordinarily attempt to produce the change all at once, and by main force. He will not rely upon extravagant promises on the one side, nor upon scolding, threats, and violence on the other. Solomon hits the idea exactly, when he speaks of "leading in the way of righteousness." We must take the young by the hand and lead them. When we have led them over the ground once, let us do it a second time, and then a third time, and so keep on, until we shall have established with them a routine, which they will continue to follow of their own accord, when the guiding hand which first led them is withdrawn. *This is training.*

The theory of it is true, not only in regard to things to be done, which is generally admitted, but also in regard to things to be known, which is often ignored if not denied. A boy, we will say, has a repugnance to the study of arithmetic. Perhaps he is particularly dull of comprehension on that subject. We shall not remove that repugnance by railing at him. We shall never make him admire it by expatiating on its beauties. It will not become clear to his comprehension by our pouring upon it all at once a sudden and overpowering blaze of light in the way of explanation. Such a process rather confounds him.

Here again let us fall back upon the method of the great Teacher, "Line upon line, precept upon precept." We will first patiently conduct our boy through one of the simplest operations of arithmetic, say, a sum in addition. The next day we will conduct him again through the same process, or through another of the same sort. The steps will gradually become familiar to his mind, then easy, then clear. He learns first the practice of arithmetic, then the rules, then the relations of numbers, then the theory on which the rules and the practice are based, and finally, he hardly knows how, he becomes an arithmetician. He has been trained into a knowledge of the subject.

You wish to teach a young child how to find a word in a dictionary. You give at first, perhaps, a verbal description of the mystery of a dictionary. You will tell him that, in such a book, all the words are arranged according to the letters with which they begin; that all the words beginning with the letter A are in the first part of the book; then those beginning with the letter B, then those beginning with C, and so on; you tell him that all the words beginning with one letter, covering some one or two hundred pages, are again re-arranged among themselves according to the second letter of each word, and then again still further re-arranged according to the third letter in each, and so on to the end. Arouse his utmost attention, and explain the process with the greatest clearness that words can give, and then set him to find a word. See how awkward will be his first attempt, how confused his ideas, how little he has really understood what you have told him. You must repeat your directions patiently, over and over, "line upon line;" you must take him by the hand day after day, and train him into a knowledge of even so apparently simple a thing as finding a word in a dictionary.

While teaching and training are thus distinguishable in theory, in practice they are well nigh inseparable. At least, they never should be separated. Teaching has never done its perfect work, until, by training, the mind has learned to run in accustomed channels, until it sees what is true, and feels what is right, with the clearness, force, and promptitude, which come only from long-continued habit.

IV.

MODES OF HEARING RECITATIONS.

THE first that I shall name is called the Concert Method. This is practised chiefly in schools for very young children, especially for those who cannot read. There are many advantages in this method, some of which are not confined to infant classes. The timid, who are frightened by the sound of their own voices when attempting to recite alone, are thereby encouraged to speak out; and those who have had any experience with such children, know that this is no small, or easy, or unimportant achievement. Another benefit of the method is the pleasure it gives the children. The measured noise and motion connected with such concert exercises, are particularly attractive to young children. Moreover, one good teacher, by the use of this method, may greatly multiply his efficiency. He may teach simultaneously fifty or sixty, instead of teaching only five or six. But in estimating this advantage, one error is to be guarded against. Visitors often hear a large class of fifty or more go through an exercise of this kind, in which the scholars have been drilled to recite in concert; and if such persons have never been accustomed to investigate the fact, they often suppose that the answers given are the intelligent responses of all the members of the class. The truth is, however, in very many such cases, that only some half dozen or so really recite the answers from their own independent knowledge. These serve as leaders; the others, sheep-like, follow. Still, by frequent repetition, even in this blind way, something gradually sticks to the memory, although the impression is always apt to be vague and undefined.

The method of reciting in concert is chiefly useful in reciting rules and definitions, or other matters, where the very words are to be committed to memory. The impression of so large a body of sound upon the ear is very strong, and is a great help in the matter of mere verbal recollection. Children too are very sympathetic, and a really skilful teacher, by the concert method, can do a great deal in cultivating the emotional nature of a large class.

Young children, too, it should be remembered, like all other young animals, are by nature restless and fidgety, and like to make a noise. It is possible, indeed, by a system of rigorous and harsh repression, to restrain this restlessness, and to keep these little ones for hours in such a state of decorous primness as not to molest weak nerves. But such a system of forced constraint is not natural to children, and is not a wise method of teaching. Let the youngsters make a noise; I had almost said, the more noise the better, so it be duly regulated. Let them exercise, not only their lungs, but their limbs, moving in concert, rising up, sitting down, turning round, marching, raising their hands, pointing to objects to which their attention is called, looking at objects which are shown to them. Movement and noise are the life of a child. They should be regulated indeed, but not repressed. To make a young child sit still and keep silence for any great length of time, is next door to murder. I verily believe it sometimes is murder. The health, and even the lives of these little ones, are sacrificed to a false theory of teaching. There is no occasion for torturing a child in order to teach him. God did not so mean it. Only let your teaching be in accordance with the wants of his young nature, and the school-room will be to him the most attractive spot of all the earth. Time and again have I seen the teacher of a primary school obliged at recess to compel her children to go out of doors, so much more pleasant did they find the school-room than the play-ground.

Quite the opposite extreme from the concert method, is that which, for convenience, may be called the individual method. In this method, the teacher examines one scholar alone upon the whole lesson, and then another, and so on, until the class is completed.

The only advantage claimed for this method is, that the individual laggard cannot screen his deficiencies, as he can when reciting in concert. He cannot make believe to know the lesson by lazily joining in with the general current of voice when the answers are given. His own individual knowledge, or ignorance, stands out. This is clear, and so far it is an advantage. But ascertaining what a pupil knows of a lesson, is only one end, and that by no means the most important end of a recitation. This interview between the pupil and teacher, called a recitation, has many ends besides that of merely detecting how much of a subject the pupil knows. A far higher end is to make him know more,—to make perfect that knowledge which the most faithful preparation on the part of the pupil always leaves incomplete.

The disadvantages of the individual method are obvious. It is a great waste of time. If a teacher has a class of twenty, and an hour to hear them in, it gives him but three minutes for each pupil, supposing there are no interruptions. But there always are interruptions. In public schools the class oftener numbers forty than twenty, and the time for recitation is oftener half an hour than an hour. The teacher who pursues the individual method to its extreme, will rarely find himself in possession of more than one minute to each scholar. In so brief a time, very little can be ascertained as to what the scholar knows of the lesson, and still less can anything be done to increase that knowledge. Moreover, while the teacher is bestowing his small modicum of time upon one scholar, all the other members of the class are idle, or worse.

Teaching, of all kinds of labor, is that in which labor-saving and time-saving methods are of the greatest moment. The teacher who is wise, will aim so to conduct a recitation that, first, his whole time shall be given to every scholar; and secondly, each scholar's mind shall be exercised with every part of the lesson, and just as much when others are reciting, as when it is his own time to recite. A teacher who can do this is teaching every scholar, all the time, just as much as if he had no scholar but that one.

Even this does not state the whole case. A scholar in such a class learns more in a given time, than he would if he were alone and the teacher's entire time were given exclusively to him. The human mind is wonderfully quickened by sympathy. In a crowd each catches, in some mysterious manner, an impulse from his fellows. The influence of associated numbers, all engaged upon the same thought, is universally to rouse the mind to a higher exercise of its powers. A mind that is dull, lethargic, and heavy in its movements when moving solitarily, often effects, when under a social and sympathetic impulse, achievements that are a wonder to itself.

The teacher, then, who knows how thus to make a unit of twenty or thirty pupils, really multiplies himself twenty or thirty-fold, besides giving to the whole class an increased momentum such as always belongs to an aggregated mass. I have seen a teacher instruct a class of forty in such a way, as, in the first place, to secure the subordinate end of ascertaining and registering with a sufficient degree of exactness how much each scholar knows of the lesson by his own preparation, and secondly, to secure, during the whole hour, the active exercise and coöperation of each individual mind, under the powerful stimulus of the social instinct, and of a keenly awakened attention. Such a teacher accomplishes more in one hour than the slave of the individual method can accomplish in forty hours. A scholar in such a class learns more in one hour than he would learn in forty hours, in a class of equal numbers taught on the other plan. Such teaching is labor-saving and time-saving, in their highest perfection, employed upon the noblest of ends.

V.

ON OBSERVING A PROPER ORDER IN THE DEVELOPMENT OF THE MENTAL FACULTIES.

EDUCATION may be defined to be the process of developing in due order and proportion all the good and desirable parts of human nature. On this point all educators are substantially agreed. Another truth, to which there is a general theoretical assent, is, that, in the order in which we develop the faculties, we should follow the leadings of nature, cultivating in childhood those faculties which seem most naturally to flourish in childish years, and reserving for maturer years the cultivation of those faculties which in the order of nature do not show much vigor until near the age of manhood, and which require for their full development a general ripening of all the other powers. The development of a human being is in some respects like that of a plant. There is one stage of growth suitable for the appearance and maturity of the leaf, another for the flower, a third for the fruit, and still a fourth for the perfected and ripened seed.

The analogy has of course many limitations. In the human plant, for instance, one class of faculties, after maturing, does not disappear in order to make place for another class, as the flower disappears before there can be fruit. Nor, again, is any class of faculties wanting altogether until the season for their development and maturity. The faculties all exist together — leaf, flower, fruit, and seed — at the same time, but each has its own best time for ripening.

While these principles have received the general assent of educators, there has been a wide divergence among them as to some of the practical applications. Which faculties do most naturally ripen early in life, and which late in life?

According to my own observation, the latest of the human powers in maturing, as it is the most consummate, is the Judgment. Next in the order of maturity, and next also in majesty and excellence, is the Reasoning power. Reason is minister to the judgment, furnishing to the latter materials for its action, as all the other powers, memory, fancy, imagination, and so forth, are ministers to reason, and supply it with its materials. The reasoning power lacks true vigor and muscle, the judgment is little to be relied on, until we approach manhood. Nature withholds from these faculties an earlier development, for the very reason, apparently, that they can ordinarily have but scanty materials for action until after the efflorescence of the other faculties. The mind must first be well filled with knowledge, which the other faculties have gathered and stored, before reason and judgment can have full scope for action.

Going to the other end of the scale, I have as little doubt that the earliest of all the faculties to bud and blossom, is the Memory. Children not only commit to memory with ease, but they take actual pleasure in it. Tasks, under which the grown-up man recoils and reels, the child will assume with light heart, and execute without fatigue. Committing to memory, which is repulsive drudgery to the man, is the easiest of all tasks to the child. More than this. The things fixed in the memory of childhood are seldom forgotten. Things learned later in life, not only are learned with greater difficulty, but more rapidly disappear. I recall instantly and without effort, texts of Scripture, hymns, catechisms, rules of grammar and arithmetic, and scraps of poetry and of classic authors, with which I became familiar when a boy. But it is a labor of Hercules for me to repeat by memory anything acquired since attaining the age of manhood. The Creator seems to have arranged an order in the natural development of the faculties for this very purpose, that in childhood and youth we may be chiefly occupied with the accumulation of materials in our intellectual storehouse. Now to reverse this process, to occupy the immature mind of childhood chiefly with the cultivation of faculties which are of later growth, and actually to put shackles and restraints upon the memory, nicknaming and ridiculing all memoriter exercises as parrot performances, is to ignore one of the primary facts of human nature. It is to be wiser than God.

Another faculty that shoots up into full growth in the very morning and spring-time of life, is Faith. I speak here, of course, not of religious belief, but of that faculty of the human mind which leads a child to believe instinctively whatever is told him. That we all do thus believe, until by slow and painful experience we learn to do otherwise, needs no demonstration. Everybody's experience attests the fact. It is equally plain that the existence and maturity of this faculty in early childhood is a most wise and beneficent provision of nature. How slow and tedious would be the first steps in knowledge, were the child born, as some teachers seem trying to make him, a sceptic, that is, with a mind which refuses to receive anything as true, except what it has first proved by experience and reason! On the contrary, how much is the acquisition of knowledge expedited, during these years of helplessness and dependency, by this spontaneous, instinctive faith of childhood. The same infinite wisdom and love, which in the order of nature provide for the helpless infant a father and mother to care for it, provide also in the constitution of the infant's mind that instinctive principle or power of faith, which alone makes the father's and mother's love efficacious towards its intellectual growth and development. Of what use were parents or teachers, in instructing a child which required proof for every statement that father, mother, or teacher gives? How cruel to force the confiding young heart into premature scepticism, by compelling him to hunt up reasons for everything, when he has reasons, to him all-sufficient, in the fact that father, mother, or teacher told him so?

It may seem trifling to dwell so long upon these elementary points. Yet there are wide-spread plans of education which violate every principle here laid down. Educators and systems of education, enjoying the highest popularity, seem to have adopted the theory, at least they tacitly act upon the theory, that the first faculty of the mind to be developed is the Reasoning power. Indeed, they are not far from asserting that the whole business of education consists in the cultivation of this power, and they bend accordingly their main energies upon training young children to go through certain processes of reasoning, so called. They require a child to prove everything before receiving it as true; to reason out a rule for himself for every process in arithmetic or grammar; to demonstrate the multiplication-table before daring to use it, or to commit it to memory, if indeed they do not forbid entirely its being committed to memory as too parrot-like and mechanical. To commit blindly to memory precious forms of truth, which the wise and good have hived for the use of the race, is poohed at as old-fogyish. To receive as true anything which the child cannot fathom, and which he has not discovered or demonstrated for himself, is denounced as slavish. All authority in teaching, growing out of the age and the reputed wisdom of the teacher, all faith and reverence in the learner, growing out of a sense of his ignorance and dependence, are discarded, and the frightened stripling is continually rapped on the knuckles, if he does not at every step show the truth of his allegations by what is called a course of reasoning. Children reason, of course. They should be encouraged and taught to reason. No teacher, who is wise, will neglect this part of a child's intellectual powers. But he will not consider this the season for its main, normal development. He will hold this subject for the present subordinate to many others. Moreover, the methods of reasoning, which he does adopt, will be of a peculiar kind, suited to the nature of childhood, the results being mainly intuitional, rather than the fruits of formal logic. To oblige a young child to go through a formal syllogistic statement in every step in elementary arithmetic, for instance, is simply absurd. It makes nothing plain to a child's mind which was not plain before. On the contrary, it often makes a muddle of what had been perfectly clear. What was in the clear sunlight of intuition, is now in a haze, through the intervening medium of logical terms and forms, through which he is obliged to look at it.

A primary teacher asks her class this question: "If I can buy 6 marbles with 1 penny, how many marbles can I buy with 5 pennies?" A bright boy who should promptly answer "30" would be sharply rebuked. Little eight-year old Solon on the next bench has been better trained than that. With stately and solemn enunciation he delivers himself of a performance somewhat of this sort. "If I can buy 6 marbles with 1 penny, how many marbles can I buy with 5 pennies? Answer—I can buy 5 times as many marbles with 5 pennies as I can buy with 1 penny. If, therefore, I can buy 6 marbles with 1 penny, I can buy 5 times as many marbles with 5 pennies; and 5 times 6 marbles are 30 marbles. Therefore, if I can buy 6 marbles with one penny, I can buy 30 marbles with 5 pennies."

And this is termed reasoning! And to train children, by forced and artificial processes, to go through such a rigmarole of words, is recommended as a means of cultivating their reasoning power and of improving their power

4

of expression! It is not pretended that children by such a process become more expert in reckoning. On the contrary, their movements as ready reckoners are retarded by it. Instead of learning to jump at once to the conclusion, lightning-like, by a sort of intuitional process, which is of the very essence of an expert accountant, they learn laboriously to stay their march by a cumbersome and confusing circumlocution of words. And the expenditure of time and toil needed to acquire these formulas of expression, which nine times out of ten are to those young minds the mere *dicta magistri*, is justified on the ground that the children, if not learning arithmetic, are learning to reason.

Let me not be misunderstood. I do not advocate the disuse of explanations. Let teachers explain, let children give explanations. Let the rationale of the various processes through which the child goes, receive a certain amount of attention. But the extreme into which some are now going, in primary education, is that of giving too much time to explanation and to theory, and too little to practice. We reverse, too, the order of nature in this matter. What it now takes weeks and months to make clear to the immature understanding, is apprehended at a later day with ease and delight at the very first statement. There is a clear and consistent philosophy underlying this whole matter. It is simply this. In the healthy and natural order of development in educating a young mind, theory should follow practice, not precede it. Children learn the practice of arithmetic very young. They take to it naturally, and learn it easily, and become very rapidly expert practical accountants. But the science of arithmetic is quite another matter, and should not be forced upon them until a much later stage in their advancement.

To have a really correct apprehension of the principle of decimal notation, for instance, to understand that it is purely arbitrary, and that we might in the same way take any other number than ten as the base of a numerical scale,—that we might increase for instance by fives, or eights, or nines, or twelves, just as well as by tens—all this requires considerable maturity of intellect, and some subtlety of reasoning. Indeed I doubt whether many of the pretentious sciolists, who insist so much on young children giving the rationale of everything, have themselves ever yet made an ultimate analysis of the first step in arithmetical notation. Many of them would open their eyes were you to tell them, for instance, that the number of fingers on your two hands may be just as correctly expressed by the figures 11, 12, 13, 14, or 15, as by the figures 10,—a truism perfectly familiar to every one acquainted with the generalizations of higher arithmetic. Yet it is up-hill work to make the matter quite clear to a beginner. We may wisely therefore give our children at first an arbitrary rule for notation. We give them an equally arbitrary rule for addition. They accept these rules and work upon them, and learn thereby the practical operations of arithmetic. The theory will follow in due time. When perfectly familiar with the practice and the forms of arithmetic, and sufficiently mature in intellect, they awaken gradually and surely, and almost without an effort, to the beautiful logic which underlies the science.

How do we learn language in childhood? Is it not

solely on authority and by example? A child who lives in a family where no language is used but that which is logically and grammatically correct, will learn to speak with logical and grammatical correctness long before it is able to give any account of the processes of its own mind in the matter, or indeed to understand those processes when explained by others. In other words, practice in language precedes theory. It should do so in other things. The parent who should take measures to prevent a child from speaking its mother tongue, except just so far and so fast as it could understand and explain the subtle logic which underlies all language, would be quite as wise as the teacher who refuses to let a child become expert in practical reckoning, until it can understand and explain at every step the rationale of the process,—who will not suffer a child to learn the multiplication table until it has mastered the metaphysics of the science of numbers, and can explain with the formalities of syllogism exactly how and why seven times nine make sixty-three.

These illustrations have carried me a little, perhaps, from my subject. But they seemed necessary to show that I am not beating the air. I have feared lest, in our very best schools, in the rebound from the exploded errors of the old system, we have unconsciously run into an error in the opposite extreme.

My positions on the particular point now under consideration may be summed up briefly, as follows:

1. In developing the faculties, we should follow the order of nature.

2. The faculties of memory and faith should be largely exercised and cultivated in childhood.

3. While the judgment and the reasoning faculty should be exercised during every stage of the intellectual development, the appropriate season for their main development and culture is near the close, rather than near the beginning, of an educational course.

4. The methods of reasoning used with children should be of a simple kind, dealing largely in direct intuitions, rather than formal and syllogistic.

5. It is a mistake to spend a large amount of time and effort in requiring young children formally to explain the rationale of their intellectual processes, and especially in requiring them to give such explanations before they have become by practice thoroughly familiar with the processes themselves.

VI.

TEACHING CHILDREN WHAT THEY DO NOT UNDERSTAND.

IT is not uncommon to hear persons declaim against teaching children what they do not understand. If by this is meant that children should not learn a set of words as parrots do, merely by the ear, and without attaching any idea to what they utter, no one will dissent from the propriety of the rule. But if the meaning is that they should learn nothing except what they fully comprehend, the rule certainly needs to be hedged in by some grave precautions.

There are indeed few things which any one, the oldest or the wisest, fully comprehends. Who knows what matter is? Certainly not the most eminent of philosophers. They do not pretend to know. We pick up a pebble. Who can tell what it is, absolutely? We say that it is something which has certain qualities. But even these we know mainly by negations. The pebble is hard, that is, it does *not* yield to pressure. It is opaque, that is, it does *not* transmit light. It is heavy, that is, it does *not* remain still, but goes towards the centre of the earth unless intercepted by some interposing body.

Who knows the meaning, absolutely, of a single article

of the Creed? Certainly not the most eminent of divines. We know certain things about the great mysteries of the Godhead, and even these things we know, not directly, but by certain faint, distant analogies, and we express our knowledge in terms chosen mainly from Scripture and arranged with care by wise and learned men. These venerable formularies, containing the most exact verbal expression which the Church has been able to frame, of what the Scriptures teach about God and his ways, we commit to memory, and we repeat them with comfort and edification. But we do not pretend to penetrate the very essence of their meaning. Who by searching can find out God? One must be God himself to understand him.

We read that Christ was tempted of the devil in the wilderness. There are many things in this transaction which we may be said, in a certain sense, to know. But a man will not proceed far in analyzing this knowledge before he will discover that there are mysteries underlying the whole, which he cannot penetrate. He knows some of the surface relations. But the things themselves, in their essence, are unknown. Was Christ tempted, as the devil tempts us, by suggesting thoughts in the mind? Was the devil present in a bodily shape? Did he utter an audible voice, by undulating the air, as we do? Has he direct relations to matter, as we have? How could his offer of worldly power and riches be any real temptation to the Saviour, when Jesus knew that Satan had no power to make his offer good?

There are indeed few things, in revelation or out of revelation, in mind or in matter, which we really and fully comprehend. If, therefore, we are to teach children nothing but what they understand, we must either teach them nothing at all, or our rule must be materially qualified. No one knows absolutely but God. Among created beings, there are almost infinite gradations of intelligence, although the highest created intelligence begins its range infinitely below that of the Divine mind. A given formula of words, therefore, may express very different degrees of truth according to the degree of intelligence of the party using it.

A catechism or a creed may convey twenty different degrees of meaning to twenty successive persons, varying in age, character, and culture. Yet the very youngest and feeblest shall understand something of its meaning, while the wisest and oldest shall not have exhausted it. The young and feeble intellect, receiving a formula of truth with suitable explanations of its terms, takes in at once a portion of its meaning and gradually grows into a fuller comprehension of what it has received. A statement of doctrine received by a child at the age of five, conveys to him a few feeble rays of light. The same statement at the age of ten, means to him far more than it did before, while at twenty it is all luminous with knowledge.

The mind itself grows and expands, and with every addition to its own vigor and stature, does it find new truths in those expressive and pregnant formulas of doctrine with which it has from childhood been familiar. It is like looking at a material object, first with the naked eye, and then with glasses of continually increased magnifying power. The more we increase the power, the more we see in the same bit of matter. Yet no glass will ever reveal to us the very interior essence of even the smallest particle of dust. God only knows fully either any single thing or the sum of things. Because, however, we cannot see into the essence of a pebble or a grain of sand, shall we shut our eyes to it altogether? Shall we not look at it, first as an infant does, then as a child, then as a youth, then as a man, then as a philosopher? We can never see it as God does. But we shall see it with ever-growing powers of vision, until that which was to us at first only a rude mass becomes an exhaustless organized microcosm of wonders.

I do not advocate the overloading of children with verbal statements of abstruse doctrines, whether of religion or of science. Much less would I turn them into parrots, to repeat phrases to which they attach no meaning at all. But when it is demanded, on the other hand, that they shall learn nothing but what they understand, I demur. I ask for explanation of the rule. I insist that, every statement of truth which they learn, even the most elementary, contains depths which neither they nor their teachers can fathom. I insist that, both in science and religion, there are certain great, admitted elementary truths, reduced to forms of sound words with which the whole world is familiar; and that while these formularies contain many things which a child cannot understand, they yet contain many things of which even the youngest child has a fair comprehension. I insist that a carefully prepared religious creed or catechism, even though it contains many things beyond a child's present comprehension, is a fit subject for study. Memory in childhood is quick and tenacious. The treasures first laid away in that great storehouse are the last to be removed. They may be overlaid by subsequent accumulations, but they are still ready for use. Forms of sound words are certainly among the things which parents and teachers should store away in the young minds of which they have charge. If the child does not understand all that he thus places in his memory, he understands portions of it just as he sees certain qualities of the pebble which he holds in his hand, and he will see and understand more, as his mind expands and his powers of spiritual vision increase.

VII.

CULTIVATING THE MEMORY IN YOUTH.

MANY educators now-a-days are accustomed to speak slightly of the old-fashioned plan of committing to memory verses of Scripture, hymns, catechisms, creeds, and other formulas of doctrine and sentiment in religion and science. Many speak disparagingly even of memory itself, and profess to think it a faculty of minor importance, regarding its cultivation as savoring of old-fogyism, and sneering at all memoriter exercises among children as the chattering of parrots. It is never without amazement that I hear such utterances. Memory is God's gift, by which alone we are able to retain our intellectual acquisitions. Without it, study is useless, and education simply an impossibility. Without it, there could be no such thing as growth in knowledge. We could know no more to-day than we knew yesterday, or last week, or last year. The man would be no wiser than the boy. Without this faculty, the mind would be, not as now like the prepared plate which the photographer puts in his camera, and which retains indelibly on its surface the impressions of whatever objects pass before it; but would rather be like the window pane, before which passes from day to day the gorgeous panorama of nature, transmitting with equal and crystalline clearness the golden glory of the sun, the pale rays of the moon and stars, the soft green of meadow and woodland, images of beauty and loveliness, of light and shade, from every object on the earth and in the heavens; but retaining on its own surface not a line or a tint of the millions of rays that have passed through its substance, and remaining to the end the same bit of transparent glass, unchanged, unprofited by the countless changes it has received and transmitted.

Memory alone gives value to the products of every other faculty, stamping them with the seal of possessorship, and making them truly ours. In vain reason forges its bolts, in vain imagination paints its scenes, in vain the senses give us a knowledge of the shapes and forms of external nature, in vain ideas of any sort or from any source come into our minds, unless we have the power to retain and fix them there, and make them a part of our accumulated intellectual wealth. To do this is the office of memory, and whatever increases the activity and power of the memory, gives at once value and growth to every other power.

Memory has been well called the store-house of our ideas. The illustration is true not only in its main feature, but in many of the minor details. The value of what a man puts away in a store-house depends much upon the order and system with which the objects are stored. The wise and thrifty merchant has bins and boxes and compartments and pigeon-holes, all arranged with due order and symmetry, and every item of goods, as it is added to his stock, is put away at once in its appropriate place, where he can lay his hands upon it whenever it is wanted. There should be a like method and system in our mental accumulations. The remembrance of facts and truths is of little value to us unless we can remember them in their connections, and can so remember them as to be able to lay our hands upon any particular thought or fact just when and where it is wanted. Many persons read and study voraciously, filling their minds most industriously with knowledge, but such a confusion of ideas prevails throughout their intellectual store-house, that their very wealth is only an embarrassment to them. The very first rule to be observed, therefore, in cultivating the memory, is to reduce our knowledge to some system. Those who are charged with the training of the young should seek not only to store their minds with ideas, but to present these ideas to them in well ordered shapes and forms, and in due logical order and coherence. Hence the peculiar value of requiring children at the proper age to commit to memory the grand formulas of Christian doctrine, on which, in every church, its wisest and ablest men have expended their strength in placing great truths in connected and logical order and dependence. The creeds and catechisms of the Christian church are among the best products of the human intellect as mere specimens of verbal statement, and are valuable, if for nothing else, as a means for exercising the memory. A child who has thoroughly mastered a good catechism has his intellectual store-house already reduced to some order and system. His mind is not the chaos that we so often find in those children who are gathered into our mission schools.

The objects that are put away for safe-keeping differ in one respect from those things which are stored away in the memory. The material object is the same, whether we visit and inspect it from day to day or not. The banker's dollars are not increased in fineness or value by his handling them over carefully every day. Not so with intellectual coin. The more frequently we re-examine our knowledge and pass it under review, the more does it become fixed in its character, the more full and exact in its proportions. Handling it does not wear it out. Even giving it away does not diminish it. In short, so far as the cultivation of the memory is concerned, the next best thing we can do, after reducing our knowledge to due order, is to give it a frequent and thorough re-examination. Constant, almost endless repetition is the inexorable price of sound mental accumulation.

A distinction is to be made between memory as a power of the mind and the remembrance of particular facts. One or two examples will illustrate this difference. The late Dr. Addison Alexander, of the Theological Seminary at Princeton, had memory as an intellectual power to a degree almost marvellous. The following instance may be cited. On one occasion, a large class of forty or fifty were to be matriculated in the Seminary in the presence of the Faculty. The ceremony of matriculation was very simple. The professors and the new students being all assembled, in a large hall, each student in turn presented himself before the professors, had his credentials examined by them, and if the same proved satisfactory, entered his name in full and his residence, in the register. When the matriculation was complete and the students had retired, there was some bantering among the professors as to which of them should take the register home and prepare from it an alphabetical roll,—a work always considered rather tedious and irksome. After a little hesitation, Dr. Alexander said, "There is no need of taking the register home; I will make the roll for you;" and, taking a sheet of paper, at once, from memory, without referring to the register, and merely from having heard the names as they were recorded, he proceeded to make out the roll, giving the names in full and giving them in their alphabetical order. This was a prodigious feat of pure memory; for in order to make the alphabetical arrangement in his mind, before committing it to paper, he must have had the entire mass of names present in his mind by a single act of the will. Some of the wonderful games of chess performed by Paul Morphy are dependent in part upon a similar power of memory, by which the player is enabled to keep present in his mind, without seeing the board, a long series of complicated evolutions, past as well as prospective and possible. The same is true of every great military strategist.

In all these cases, there is an act of pure memory, a direct and positive power of summoning into the mind its past experiences, such as can only take place where, either by natural gift or by special training, the memory as a faculty of the mind is in a high state of vigor. But there are other cases, in which a man is enabled to recall a great number of particular facts by a species of artifice or trick, which does not imply any special mental power, and the study of which does not tend, in any marked degree, to develop such power. More than thirty years ago, the late Professor Dod, of Princeton College, in lecturing to a class on the subject of light, was explaining the solar spectrum, and after exhibiting the solar ray, divided into its seven primary colors, violet, indigo, blue, green, yellow, orange, and red, said, "If you will form a mnemonic word of the first letters of each of these words, you will be able, without further effort, to remember the order of the prismatic colors the rest of your lives," and he accordingly wrote upon the board and pronounced the uncouth and almost unpronounceable word, *Vibgyor,* which probably not one of us has ever forgotten. An ingenious Frenchman some years ago traversed the country and collected large audiences by his exhibitions of skill in this species of artifice, and by undertaking to initiate his hearers in the method of remembering prodigious numbers of historical facts by means of such artificial contrivances. Mnemotechny, the name which he gave to his invention, is merely a trick of the memory. It is a means of remembering a particular set of facts or things by the aid of contrivances purely artificial and arbitrary. Its possession does not imply, and its cultivation does not produce, real mnemonic power. It undoubtedly has its uses. But it is rather wealth gained by a lottery ticket than a wealth-producing power acquired by wise habits of business.

In teaching the young, it is well not to neglect either of these principles. We should give our children from time to time ingenious and interesting contrivances for remembering important facts. These contrivances, if judicious in plan and execution, will be great helps to them. We may in this way bridge over the difficulty of remembering many of the important facts and dates in history.

I would not discourage these artificial methods. Though they are mere tricks, they are valuable. But they have by no means the same value as those methods of teaching which cultivate and produce true mnemonic power. This power, like every other mental power, is given in unequal measure to different individuals. Like every other mental power, also, it grows mainly by exercise. No power of the mind is more capable of development. I have mentioned some things which tend to the growth of this power, such as presenting knowledge to children in logical and orderly arrangement, and frequent re-examination of knowledge already obtained. Perhaps there is no quickener and invigorator of the memory equal to that of reciting to a judicious teacher before a large class of fellow-students. By a proper and skilful use of the art of questioning, under the excitement of answering before a large class, the mnemonic power is subjected to a healthy and invigorating test, and all such exercises promote powerfully the mental growth. A child may absorb knowledge by mere solitary reading and study, just as a sponge absorbs water, but the knowledge so acquired readily evaporates, or is squeezed out. Something is needed to fix in the mind the knowledge that has been lodged there, and no process is more effectual to this end than that of class recitation. It is by telling other people what we have learned, that we learn it more effectually, and make it more completely our own. A good teacher, by good methods of recitation, can do more than all other persons and all other things to secure a sound and healthy growth of memory in the young.

Another thing highly necessary in cultivating a really good memory, is attaining the utmost possible clearness in our ideas. If the knowledge, when it first comes into the mind, is clearly and sharply defined, so that we really know a thing, instead of having vague and confused notions about it, we shall be the more likely to remember it permanently. Nothing is more conducive towards giving these sharp and definite impressions than the use of visible illustrations. Actual exhibition before a class of the objects talked about, actual experiments of the operations described, and the constant use of the chalk and the black-board, presenting even abstract truths in concrete and visible symbols, as is done in algebra, chemistry, and logic, are among the means by which, chiefly, knowledge becomes well defined to the mind. Such is the constitution of the mind, that we have a clearer apprehension of what we see than of what comes to us through any other sense, and the knowledge which comes to us by means of the sight, is, of all kinds of knowledge, the most lasting and the most easily recalled. Hence, in teaching, it is hardly possible to exaggerate the importance of visible illustration.

Another condition extremely favorable to the growth of memory, is the existence of a considerable degree of mental excitement at the time that knowledge enters the mind. Metals weld easily only at a white heat. If we would obtain a vigorous grasp of knowledge, and incorporate it thoroughly into our other mental products, so that it shall become really ours, there should be the glow of mental heat at the time of our acquiring such knowledge. Ideas that come into the mind when we are in an apathetic state, make no permanent lodgment. Hence the importance of exciting a lively interest in that which is the subject of study. If the teacher has failed to excite this interest, and finds in his class no animation, no sympathy, no eagerness of attention, he may be sure that he is not accomplishing much. The child must, if possible, acquire a fondness for that which is to be remembered. Love, in fact, is the parent of memory.

VIII.

KNOWLEDGE BEFORE MEMORY.

I HAVE had frequent occasion to urge upon teachers the importance of cultivating the memory of their pupils. The old-fashioned plan of requiring the young to commit to memory precious truths, in those very words in which wise and far-thinking men have handed them down to us, has too much gone out of use. I have felt called upon, therefore, from time to time, to recall to the minds of teachers the unspeakable importance of early exercising the memory of children, and of storing their memories with wise sayings and rules. I would not take back anything I have said on this subject, but rather repeat and reiterate it. At the same time, I am aware that there is an extreme in this direction, and I therefore put in a word of caution.

The danger to which I refer is that of requiring children to commit mere words, to which they attach no meaning, or without their having any real knowledge of the things expressed by the words. Of course there is much in the formulas and rules of science that the immature minds of children cannot entirely comprehend, and I am far from saying that a child should commit nothing except what it can comprehend. But whatever in a rule or a doctrine they can understand, should be diligently explained to them, and the ingenuity of teachers should be exercised in awakening the minds of their scholars to the apprehension of real knowledge as a preliminary to the act of committing it to memory.

An example or two will illustrate my meaning. Children at school are required to commit to memory the tables of weights and measures. The exercise is one of acknowledged and indispensable importance. But it is possible for a child to repeat one of these tables with entire glibness and accuracy, pretty much as he would whistle Yankee Doodle, without any apprehension of the actual things which the terms of the table represent. He may learn to say "sixty seconds make a minute, sixty minutes make a degree, three hundred and sixty degrees make a circle," with no more idea of the things expressed by this formula of words, than the parrot who has been taught to say, "You are a big fool." If the teacher will show the child an actual circle, with the degrees, minutes, and seconds marked, and will let him count them for himself, so that he has a real knowledge of the things, he will then not only commit this formula of words to memory more easily, but the knowledge itself will promote his mental growth. He will be feeding on real knowledge, not on its husks. So in learning about inches, feet, yards, rods, and miles, let the teacher, with foot-rule and yard-stick, show what these measures really are, let him by some familiar instance give the child an idea of what a mile is, and then let the memory be invoked to store up the knowledge gained. So with ounces, pounds. and hundred-weights.

So with gills, quarts, and gallons. The common weights and measures are as necessary in the school-room as are spelling-books and arithmetics. The actual weights and measures, so far as possible, should be exhibited, should be seen and handled, and the child's mind made to grasp the very things which the terms express, that is, he should first get real knowledge, and then he should store his memory with it in exact words and forms of expression.

This is the true mental order. Knowledge first, then memory. Get knowledge, then keep it. Any other plan is like attempting to become rich by inflating your bags with wind, instead of filling them with gold, or attempting to grow fat by bolting food in a form which you cannot digest.

Some teachers, in their fear of cramming children with words, spend their whole time and energy in awakening thought, and none in fixing upon the memory the thoughts which have been awakened. They are so much afraid of making children parrots, that they discard rules entirely in teaching, or require pupils to frame rules for themselves. This is to go into the opposite extreme. The rules and formulas of science require the greatest care and consideration, and a large and varied knowledge. Few even of men of learning and of those specially skilled in the meaning of words and the use of language, are qualified to frame scientific rules and propositions. To suppose that young children, just beginning to feel their way into any department of science, are competent to such a task, is simply absurd. Yet this is by no means uncommon.

A teacher will conduct a boy intelligently and skilfully through the process of doing a sum in arithmetic, or analyzing a sentence in grammar, and then say to him, "Now, form a rule for yourself, stating how such things should be done." The first step here is right. Take your pupil by the hand, and conduct him through the process or thing to be done. This is necessary to enable him to understand the rule. But when he thus gets the idea, then give him the rule or principle, as it is laid down in the book, in exact and well considered words, and let him commit those words thoroughly to memory, without the change or the omission of a word or a letter.

What is thus true as to the method of teaching the common branches of knowledge, is equally true in the study of religious knowledge. I would not set a child to framing a creed or a catechism, nor, on the other hand, would I require him to commit such formulas to memory, without making some attempt to awaken in his mind previously an apprehension of the ideas which the creed or formula contains. I do not say that a child's mind is competent to grasp all the truths embraced in these symbols. But there is no portion of any religious creed or catechism that I have ever seen, some of the terms of which are not capable of being apprehended by children. A wise teacher, in undertaking to indoctrinate a child in such a formula, will begin by showing him as far as possible what the words mean, by exciting in him ideas on the subject, by filling his mind with actual knowledge of the truths contained in the formula. Then, when the words of the formula have become to the child's mind instinct with meaning and life, the teacher will pause to stamp them in upon the memory. That is the way to study a catechism. First, give the child, so far as possible, the meaning, then grind the words into him. Do not set him to making a catechism; do not let him stop at understanding the meaning, without committing the words.

Two phrases will cover the whole ground. Knowledge before memory. Memory as well as knowledge.

IX.

THE POWER OF WORDS.

WORDS govern the world. Let any one who doubts it, canvass the motives by which his own action is decided. Considerations are presented to his mind, showing him that a certain course of conduct is right, or good, or expedient, or pleasant, and he adopts it. The considerations presented to his mind decide his action. But those considerations are in the form of arguments, and those arguments exist in words. The true original power, indeed, is in the thought. It is the thinker who generates the steam. But thought unexpressed accomplishes nothing. The writer and the speaker engineer it into action.

Thought, indeed, even in the mind of its originator, exists in words. For we really think only in words. Much more, then, must the thought have some verbal expression, written or spoken, before it can influence the opinions or the actions of others. A man may have all the wisdom of Solomon, yet will he exercise no influence upon human affairs unless he gives his wisdom utterance. Profound thinkers sometimes, indeed, utter very little. But they must utter something. They originate and give forth a few thoughts or discoveries, which minds of a different order, writers and talkers, pick up, reproduce, multiply, and disseminate all over the surface of society. When a man unites these two functions, being both an original thinker and a skilful and industrious writer, the influence which he may exert upon his race is prodigious. If any one, for instance, would take the pains to trace the influences which have sprung from such a man as Plato, he would have an illustration of what is meant. Plato, while living, had no wealth, rank, or position of any kind, to add force to what he said or did. Whatever he has done in the world, he has done simply by his power as a thinker and a writer. There were many Grecians quite as subtle and acute in reasoning as he. But their thoughts died with them. Plato, on the other hand, was an indefatigable writer, as well as an acute and profound thinker. He gave utterance to his ideas in words which, even in a dead language, have to this day a living power. When Plato was dead, there remained his written words. They remain still. They have entered successively into the philosophies, the creeds, and the practical codes, of the Grecian world, the Roman, the Saracen, and the Christian. At this very hour hundreds of millions of human beings unconsciously hold opinions which the words of that wise old Greek have helped to mould. The mere brute force of a military conqueror may make arbitrary changes in the current of human affairs. But no permanent change is ever made except by the force of opinion. The words of Plato have done more to influence the destinies of men than have a hundred such men as Genghis Khan or Tamerlane. Four hundred millions of Chinese, in half the actions which go to make up their lives, are now governed by maxims and opinions which have come down to them from remote antiquity, from a man whose very existence is almost a myth. Those military heroes whose influence on society has been permanent have been propagandists as well as warriors. Opinions and codes have gone with, and survived, their conquering armies. The armies of the elder Napoleon were routed at Waterloo. But the Napoleonic ideas survived the shock, and they are at this day a part of the governing power of the world. It was the Koran — the words, and the creed of Mahomet — that gave to the Mahometan conquest its permanent hold upon the nations.

Spoken words have in themselves greater power than merely written ones. There is a wonderful influence in the living voice to give force and emphasis to what is uttered. But the written word remains. What is lost in immediate effect, is more than gained in the permanent result. The successful writer has an audience for all time. He being dead still speaks. Men are speaking now, who have gone to their final account twenty centuries ago. Paul possibly may not have had the same influence with a popular assembly as the more eloquent Apollos. But Paul is speaking still through his ever-living Epistles. He is speaking daily to more than a hundred millions of human beings. He is exerting through his writings a power incomparably greater than that even which he exercised as a living speaker.

All men have not the commanding gifts of the apostle Paul. Yet after all, the main difference between ordinary men and men of the Pauline stamp, is not so much in their natural powers, as in the spirit and temper of the men, in that entire consecration to the service of Christ which Paul had, and which they have not. It is wonderful to see how much may be accomplished even by men of ordinary talents, when they have that zeal and single-mindedness which may be attained by one as well as by another. We are accountable for the talents which we have, not for what we have not. But let each man see to it that he uses to the utmost every talent which his Lord has committed to his trust.

How much, for instance, may be accomplished by a man who has a gift for addressing a popular assembly! Such a man by a few wise words, spoken at the right time and place, may do as much in five minutes, in pushing forward a general cause, as another man can do by the laborious drudgery of years. The words of the speaker touch the secret springs of action in a thousand breasts. He sends away a thousand men and women animated with a new impulse to duty, and that impulse is propagated and reproduced through hundreds of channels for long years to come.

Words are never entirely idle. They have at times a power like that of the electric bolt. They may sting like a serpent, and bite like an adder. In the ordinary intercourse of society, a man of good conversational powers may, even in discharging the customary civilities of life, put forth a large influence. The words dropped from minute to minute, throughout the day, in the millions of little transactions all the while going on between man and man, have an incalculable power in the general aggregate of the forces which keep society in motion.

As with spoken, so with written words. The man who knows how to weave them into combinations which shall gain the popular ear, and sink into the popular heart, has a mighty gift for good or evil. The self-denying and almost saintly Heber, by all his years of personal toil on the plains of India, did not accomplish a tithe of what has been accomplished for the cause of missions by his one Missionary Hymn. It would hardly be an exaggeration to say that those few written words are worth more to the cause than the lives of scores of ordinary missionaries. How many anxious souls, just wavering between a right and a wrong decision, have been led to make the final choice, and to decide for Christ, by that beautiful hymn beginning "Just as I am, without one plea"? Who can doubt that the patient invalid of Torquay, in the hour that she penned those touching words, did more for the conversion of sinners than many a minister of the gospel has done in the course of a long and laborious life? What a fund of consolation for pious hearts through all time is laid up in the hymns of that other sweet singer, Mrs. Steele?

But as with spoken, so with written words, the great aggregate of their force is not contained in these few brilliant and striking exceptions, but in the millions of mere ordinary paragraphs which meet the eye from day to day, in the columns of the daily and weekly press, and which have apparently but an ephemeral existence. The dashing torrent and the mighty river are the more noticeable objects to the casual observer. But it is the minute myriad drops of the rain and the dew that cause the real wonders of vegetation. So these words which we read, and think we forget, hour by hour, all day long, are continually sinking into the soil of the heart, and influencing imperceptibly the growth of the germs of thought. The aggregate of all these minute, unnoticed influences is prodigious, incalculable.

Whoever can put words together wisely, either by the tongue or the pen, has a precious talent, which he may not innocently lay up in a napkin. The gift, like that of wealth, is not his by right of ownership, but only as a steward. It is his as a means to do good for the honor of his Lord, and the welfare of his fellow-men. As I said in the beginning of these remarks, the world is governed by words. Let Christian men, by the industrious use of the gifts they have received, see to it that a greater proportion of this governing force in the world is contributed by the friends of Christ. Let them unceasingly fill up with the words of truth and righteousness every accessible channel of thought and opinion, and thus occupy till Christ come.

X.

THE STUDY OF LANGUAGE.

THE study of language has ever been considered a study of high importance, regarded merely as a means of intellectual cultivation.

There are obvious reasons for this. The analysis of language is the analysis of thought. Resolving complex forms of speech into simple ones, and again combining simple expressions into those which are complex, and investigating, alternately by logic and æsthetics, the varying properties of words and phrases, are operations which come nearer, perhaps, than any other in which we are engaged, towards subjecting spirit itself to the crucible of experiment. The study of grammar, the comparison of languages, the translation of thought from one language to another, are so many studies in logic and the laws of mind. The subtleties of language arise from the very nature of that subtle and mysterious essence, the human mind, of which speech is the prime agent and medium of communication.

The class of studies under consideration bears nearly the same relation to the spiritual that anatomy does to the bodily part of us. It is by the dissecting-knife of a keen and well-tempered logic, applied to the examination of the various forms which human thought assumes, that we most truly learn the very essence and properties of thought itself. It is this intimate, immediate, indissoluble connection and correlation between mind and language, between human thought and human speech, between the soul itself and the mould into which it is cast, that gives such importance to the general class of studies known as philological.

The study of language, more than any other study, tends to make the mind acute, discriminating, and exact. It tends also, in a most especial manner, to fit a person to train the minds of others to acuteness, discrimination, and exactness. The person who has learned to express a thought with entire exactness and idiomatic propriety in two languages; or where, from the want of analogy between the two languages, he finds this impracticable, to perceive the exact shade of difference between the two expressions; who can trace historically and logically the present meaning of a word from its original starting-point in reason and fact, and mark intelligently its gradual departures and their causes; who can perceive the exact difference between words and phrases nearly synonymous, and who can express that difference in terms clear and intelligible to others, — that person has already attained both a high degree of intellectual acumen himself, and an important means of producing such acumen in others.

The study of language is, in the profession of teaching, like the sharpening of tools in the business of the mechanic. Words are the teacher's tools. Human knowledge, even before it is expressed, and as it is laid up in the chambers of the mind, exists in words. We think in words. We teach in words. We are qualified to teach only so far as we have learned the use and power of words.

XI.

CULTIVATING THE VOICE.

IF we except the lower kinds of handicraft, nine-tenths of all that is done in the world is done by means of the voice,—by talking. It is by talking we buy and sell; by talking, the lawyer, the doctor, the minister, the teacher perform the chief of their functions; by talking, the intercourse and machinery of life are chiefly kept in motion. As it was by a word that creation was accomplished, as the worlds came into being and were moulded into shape, not by the hand, but by the omnific voice of God, *saying*, "Let there be light and there was light," so in this lower sphere of human action, the tongue is mightier than the hand. The moulding, propelling forces of society come from the use of words. By words, more than by all other means, we persuade, convince, alarm, arouse, or soothe, or whatever else leads men to action and achievement; and while written words are full of power, yet even these are feeble as compared with spoken words, the living utterances of the human voice. Not only so, but the manner of speaking, the tone and quality of the voice influence us quite as much as the words spoken.

Yet how strangely we neglect this wonderful instrument. The mechanic sees to it that his tools are as keen and strong as it is in the power of art and labor to make them. The sportsman spares no expense or care to have the articles that minister to his pleasure in the highest possible state of finish and perfection. How lavish we are in the purchase of instruments of music, and in keeping them properly tuned and cared for. Yet this most wonderful organ, the voice, which God has given to every one of us, and which is worth more to us than all the instruments of music, all the inventions of pleasure, all the tools of trade, that human skill has devised, is left for the most part in utter neglect, without intelligent guidance, its wonderful powers almost totally uncultivated and undeveloped. We all feel the sway that a well cultivated and modulated voice has upon us, its power to give us pleasure and win our assent, and yet the great majority of us neglect to cultivate in ourselves that which may give us such a power over others. We are not oblivious of other advantages. We strive to make ourselves acceptable and to increase our influence, by attention to dress, by the adornment of our persons, and by the cultivation of our minds, by stores of knowledge and by accomplishments of various kinds, while the voice, which more than anything else is the direct instrument of the soul, is treated with neglect.

We mumble and mutter what should come out clearly and distinctly; we speak with a nasal drawl, or in a sharp key that sets all the finer chords of sympathy ajar; we use just so much of the vocal power that is given us as is needed to express in the faintest way our most imperative wants, and indolently leave all the rest of its untold and exquisite resources to go to waste.

Mrs. Siddons once made a shopkeeper turn pale with affright and unconsciously drop his goods upon the counter, simply by the tone in which, by way of experiment, she asked him the price of a pair of gloves. Undoubtedly Mrs. Siddons had natural gifts of voice which do not belong to every one. But a great part of the wonderful fascination which she and the other members of that remarkable family exerted, was due to cultivation.

If ministers of the gospel, and others who undertake to influence the minds of a congregation on the side of religion, would give this matter more attention, they would find it very greatly to their own advantage and that of others. The manner in which the words of eternal life are read and uttered from the pulpit is often such as to kill all vitality out of them. It is not enough that a preacher should be a good theologian, and that his sermon contain sound and valuable thoughts. The influence which they are to exert upon the people, is largely dependent upon the voice which gives them utterance. A competent teacher of elocution is quite as important a part of the machinery of a theological seminary, as a teacher of Hebrew. Yet, in organizing our seminaries, this matter is usually entirely ignored.

XII.

EYES.

I HAVE spoken much of blackboards, maps, pictorial cards, natural objects, and apparatus of various kinds, as among the urgent wants of the teacher. But there is one thing which he wants more than all these, and that is EYES. A good pair of eyes are to the teacher, in the government of his school, worth more than the rod, more than any system of merit or demerit marks, more than keeping in after school, more than scolding, reporting to parents, suspension, or expulsion, more than coaxing, premiums, and bribes in any shape or to any amount. The very first element in school government, as in every other government, is that the teacher should know what is going on in his little kingdom, and for this knowledge he needs a pair of eyes.

Most teachers, it is true, seem to be furnished with this article. But it is in appearance only. They have something in the upper part of the face which looks like eyes, but every one knows that appearances are deceiving. They look over a school or an assembly of any kind, and are vaguely conscious that things are going on wrong all around them, just as people sometimes grope about in a dark room filled with bats, and are aware that something is flitting about, but they have no power of seeing distinctly any one object. It is amazing how little some people see, who seem to have eyes.

The fact is, there is an entirely mistaken notion on this whole subject. Having the eyes open, and seeing, are two distinct things. Infants have their eyes open, but they do not see anything, in the sense in which that word is generally used. Light comes into those open windows, the moving panorama of external nature passes before them, but distinct vision, which recognizes and individualizes objects, is something more than a mere passive, bodily sensation. It is a mental act. It is the mind rousing itself into consciousness, and putting forth its powers into voluntary and self-determined activity. Nothing in the history of childhood is more interesting than to watch this awakening of the mind in infancy, to notice how the whole face brightens up when the little stranger first begins actually to see things.

The misfortune with many people is, that in this matter of vision they seem never to get beyond the condition of infancy. They go along the street, or they move about in a room, in a sort of dreamy state, their eyes open, but seeing nothing. A teacher of this kind, no matter what amount of disorder is going on before him, never sees any one particular act. He sees things in the mass, instead of seeing individual things. The difference between teachers in this faculty of seeing things is more marked probably than in any other quality that a man can have. Two teachers may stand before the same class. One will merely be aware that there is a general disorder and noise throughout, being unable to identify any scholar in particular as transgressing. The other will notice that John is talking, that James is pulling his neighbor's hair, that William is drumming on the desk with his fingers, that Andrew is munching an apple, that Peter is making caricatures on his slate, and so on.

To have this power of seeing things, it is not necessary that one should be sly, or should use stealth of any kind. Knowledge gained by such mean practices never amounts to much, and always lowers a teacher in the estimation of his scholars; it weakens instead of strengthening him. Whatever a teacher does in the way of observation of his scholars, should be done openly and aboveboard. And after all, more can be seen in this way, by one who knows how, than by any of the stealthy practices usually resorted to. Darting the eyes about rapidly in one direction and another, is not a good way to make discoveries. Seeing is accomplished, not so much by the activity of the bodily organ, as by mental activity. The man's mind must be awake. This in fact is the secret of the whole matter. The more the face and eyes are quiet, and the mind is on the alert, the more a man will see. Seeing is rather a mental than a bodily act, though of course the bodily organ is necessary to its accomplishment. To be a good observer, one must maintain a quiet and composed demeanor, but be thoroughly wide awake within.

XIII.

ERRORS OF THE CAVE.

IMPROVEMENT comes by comparison. One of the most profound observations of Bacon is that in which he remarks upon the dwarfing and distorting influence of solitariness upon the human faculties. The man who shuts himself up in his own little circle of thought and action as in a cave, having no consort with his fellows, evolving all his plans from his own solitary cogitation, must be more than human if he does not become one-sided, narrow, selfish, bigoted.

A like result, but not so aggravated, is produced, when a man limits his range of thought and action to those of his own special calling or profession; when the merchant mingles only with merchants and knows only merchandise; when the teacher knows nothing but teaching and books; when the medical man spends every waking hour and every active exercise of thought upon his healing art; when any man forgets that, in the very fact of his being a man at all, he is something greater and nobler than he can possibly be in being merely a merchant, or teacher, or doctor, or lawyer, or the possessor of any other one special art or faculty.

It is true, indeed, that in order to attain to eminence in

any one department, a man must bend his main energies to that one thing; and he must give to it much solitary thought and study. But no department of action is isolated. No interest is unconnected with other interests. No truth stands alone, but forms a part in the great system of truth. Study or action, therefore, which is entirely isolated, must needs be dwarfed and distorted.

A man must go occasionally out of his own sphere in order fully to understand those very things with which he is most familiar. A man must study other languages, if he would hope fully to understand his own. A man must study more than languages merely if he would become a perfect linguist. The only way to understand arithmetic thoroughly is to study algebra. A parent who has only one child, and who gives his entire and exclusive attention to the study of that child, in order that he may, by a thorough understanding of its nature and disposition, be better able to teach and train it, will not be so likely to attain his object as he would if he were to spend a portion of his time in mingling with other children and in becoming acquainted with childhood generally. A teacher who should shut himself up in his own school-room, giving to it every moment of his waking hours, would not be likely to benefit so largely his own pupils, as if he were to spend a portion of his time in communing with other teachers and observing other methods besides his own. A teacher even who should mingle freely with those of his own profession, and get all the benefit to be derived from observation of the views and methods of other teachers, but should stop there, would not yet obtain that broad, comprehensive view, even of his own calling, and of the duties of his own particular school-room that he might have if he would travel occasionally beyond the walk of books and pedagogy, and become acquainted with the views and methods of men in other spheres of life, with merchants, lawyers, and doctors, with farmers, mechanics, and artisans.

It is only by mingling with those outside of our own little specialty that we are disenthralled from the bonds of prejudice. It is wonderful to see the change produced in the minds of men of different religious denominations, when by any means they are thrown much into the actual fellowship of working together in some cause of common benevolence. How, without any argument, merely by the fact of their being brought out to a different point of view, the relative magnitude and importance of certain truths change in their estimation! The points in which Christians differ become so much smaller; the points in which they agree become so much larger. The little stone at the mouth of the cave no longer hides the mountain in the distance.

Let the teacher, the merchant, the mechanic, the banker, the lawyer, the minister of religion even, still remember that he is a man, and that he can never reach a full and just estimate of his own position without sometimes going outside of it and placing himself in the position of other men.

XIV.

MEN OF ONE IDEA.

THERE is between the teacher and other operatives one obvious difference, arising from the difference in the materials upon which their labor is bestowed. That class of laborers whose toil and skill are exerted in modifying the forms of matter, succeed generally in proportion to the narrowness of the range to which each individual's attention is confined. It is possible (the writer has known it to be a fact) for the same person to sow the flax, to pull and rot it, to break it, hatchel it, spin it, warp it, weave it, dye or bleach it, and finally make it into clothes. I say this is *possible*, for I have seen it done, and I dare say many of my readers have seen the same. But how coarse and expensive is such a product, compared with that in which every step in the progress of production is made the subject of one individual's entire and undivided attention.

If we were to go into the factories of Lowell, or into any of the thousand workshops which are converting Philadelphia into a great manufacturing centre, we would find the manufacture of an article approaching perfection just in proportion to the *im*perfection (in one sense) of the individual workmen employed in its production. The man who can make a pin-head better and cheaper than any one else, must give his attention to making pin-heads only. He need not know how to point a pin, or polish it, or cut the wire. On the contrary his skill in that one operation increases ordinarily in proportion to his want of skill in others. His perfection as a workman is in the direct ratio to his imperfection as a man. He operates upon matter, and the more nearly he can bring his muscles and his volitions to the uniformity and the precision of a mere machine — the more confined, monotonous, and undeviating are his operations — the higher is the price set upon his work, the better is he fitted for his task.

Not so the instructor of youth. The material operated on here is of a nature too subtle to be shaped and fashioned by the undeviating routine of any such mechanical operations. The process necessary to sharpen one intellect may terrify and confound another. The means which in one instance serve to convince, serve in other cases to confuse. The illustration which to one is a ray of light, is to another only "darkness visible." Mind is not, like matter, fixed and uniform in its operations. The workman who is to operate upon a substance so subtle and so varying must not be a man of *one idea* — who knows one thing, and nothing more. It is not true in mind, as in matter, that perfection in the knowledge of one particular point is gained by withdrawing the attention from every other point. All truth and all knowledge are affiliated. The knowledge of arithmetic is increased by that of algebra, the knowledge of geography by that of astronomy, the knowledge of one language by knowing another. As no one thing in nature exists unconnected with other things, so no one item in the vast sum of human knowledge is isolated, and no person is likely to be perfectly acquainted with any one subject who confines his attention with microscopic minuteness to that subject. To understand thoroughly one subject, you must study it not only in itself, but in its relations. To know one thing well you must know very many other things.

Let us return then to the point from which we set out, namely: that one important difference between the teacher and other operatives arises from the difference in the objects on which they operate. The one operates upon matter, the other upon mind. The one attains perfection in his art by a process which in the other would produce an ignoramus, a bungler, a narrow-minded, conceited charlatan. Hence the necessity on the part of those who would excel in the profession of teachers, of endeavoring continually to enlarge the bounds of their knowledge. Hence the error of those who think that to teach anything well it is necessary to know only that one thing. That young woman who undertakes to teach a primary school, or even an infant class, has mistaken her calling if she supposes that because she has to teach only the alphabet or the "table card," she has therefore no need to know many other things. There are some things which every teacher needs. Every teacher needs a cultivated taste, a disciplined intellect, and that enlargement of views which results only from enlarged knowledge.

We all know how much we are ourselves benefited by associating habitually with persons of superior abilities.

So it is in a still higher degree with children. There is something contagious in the fire of intellect. The human mind, as well as the human heart, has a wonderful power of assimilation. Every judicious parent will say: Let not my child be consigned to the care of an ill-informed, dull, spiritless teacher. Let it be his happy lot, if possible, to be under one who has some higher ambition than merely to go through a certain prescribed routine of duties and lessons; one whose face beams with intelligence and whose lips drop knowledge; one who can cultivate in him the disposition to inquire, by his own readiness and ability to answer childish inquiries; who can lead the inquiries of a child into proper channels, and train him to a correct mode of thinking by being himself familiar with the true logical process, by having himself a cultivated understanding. Such a teacher finds a pleasure in his task. He finds that he is not only teaching his pupils to read and to spell, to write and to cipher, but he is acquiring an ascendancy over them. He is exerting upon them a moral and intellectual power. He is leaving, upon a material far more precious than any coined in the Mint, the deep and inerasible impress of his own character.

Let me repeat then, at the risk of becoming tiresome, what I hold to be an important and elementary truth, that the teacher should know very many things besides what he is required to teach. A good knowledge of history will enable him to invest the study of geography with new interest. Acquaintance with algebra will give a clearness to his perceptions, and consequently to his mode of inculcating the principles, of arithmetic. The ability to delineate off-hand with chalk or pencil the forms of objects, gives him an unlimited power of illustrating every subject, and of clothing even the dullest with interest. Familiarity with the principles of rhetoric and with the rules of criticism, gives at once elegance and ease to his language, and the means of more clearly detecting what is faulty in the language of others. A knowledge of Latin or of French, or of any language besides his own, throws upon his own language a light of which he before had no conception. It produces in his ideas of grammar and of language generally, a change somewhat like that which the anatomist experiences from the study of comparative anatomy. The student of the human frame finds many things that he cannot comprehend until he extends his inquiries to other tribes of animals; to the monkey, the ox, the reptile, the fish, and even to the insect world. So it is with language. We return from the study of a foreign language invariably with an increased knowledge of our own. We have made one step at least from the technicalities of particular rules towards the principles and truths of general grammar.

But it is not necessary to multiply illustrations. I have already said enough to explain my meaning. Let me say, then, to every teacher, as you desire to rise in your profession, as you wish to make your task agreeable to yourself or profitable to your pupils, do not cease your studies as soon as you gain your election, but continue to be a learner as long as you continue to be a teacher, and especially strive by all proper means, and at all times, to enlarge the bounds of your knowledge.

XV.

A TALENT FOR TEACHING.

THERE can be no doubt that some persons have a natural aptitude for teaching. As there are born poets, so there are born teachers. Yet the man born with the true poetic temperament and faculty will never achieve success as a poet, unless he add study and labor to his natural gift. So the man born with a talent for teaching needs to cultivate the talent by patient study and practice, before he can become a thoroughly accomplished teacher. No man probably ever showed greater native aptitude for anything, than did Benjamin West for painting. Yet what long years of toil and study it took for him to become a really great painter? In teaching, as in every other profession, while men doubtless differ as to their original qualifications and aptitudes, yet the differences are not so great as they are often supposed to be, and they are by no means so great as those produced by study and practice. The man who has no special gift for this employment, but who faithfully and intelligently tries to perfect himself in it, is sure to be a better teacher than the one who has the natural gift, but adds to it no special study and preparation. Indeed, if we exclude from consideration those very nice and delicate touches in education, which are so rare as to be quite exceptional, there is nothing in the business of teaching which may not be acquired by any person of average ability.

When, therefore, we see a teacher not succeeding in gaining the attention of his scholars, or in securing obedience and respect, or in bringing them forward in their lessons, we are not disposed to free such a person from blame on the plea of his having no natural aptitude for teaching. We would respectfully say to such a teacher: if you know not how to impart knowledge, learn how; if you have no tact, get it. Teaching is a business, as much as knitting stockings, or planting corn. Either do not undertake to teach at all, or learn how it is to be done.

If one-fourth of the labor bestowed upon the work of teaching were devoted to studying the business, the value of the remaining three-fourths would be quadrupled. It is painful to see the amount of hard work done in school with so little proportionate effect. If a man who knew nothing of farming, but who had a desire to be useful, were to dig a pit and bury therein a bushel of corn, and imagine that he was planting, his labor would not be wider of the mark than much that is bestowed in school. A man must learn how to do even so simple a thing as planting corn. Let the teacher also learn how to plant the seeds of knowledge, how to prepare the soil, how to open it for the reception of truth, where and when to deposit the precious grains.

I have no desire to discourage those faithful men and women who are so nobly striving to do good as teachers. But I cannot help expressing the regret that so much of this labor is without adequate result. Why should persons act so differently in this matter from what they do in any other? If a woman wants to make a pair of stockings, she goes to some other woman who understands knitting, and sees how it is done, and learns the stitches, tries and experiments, and studies the matter, until it is all familiar to her. So of any other ordinary business. Yet when it comes to teaching, anything like definite study or observation of the mode of doing it, is almost unknown! It is really no exaggeration to say that many teachers bungle in their work as egregiously as would a woman who should put yarn into a churn, and expect, after a proper amount of churning, to draw out stockings.

In our schools are many professional teachers of approved skill. Why should not a school-teacher, who is conscious of not succeeding as he would desire, spend an hour occasionally in observation? Find out the name of some teacher who is particularly successful, and look on while the work is being done, and if possible see how it is done.

Then again, there are books on the subject, in which the business of teaching is explained in all its branches. Get some of these books and read. The mere reading will not make you teachers. But it will set you to thinking. It will quicken your power of observation. It will help you to learn from your own experience.

Make a note of the difficulties you encounter, and the points in which you cannot accomplish what you desire. Very likely you will find these very difficulties discussed in the books on teaching which you are reading. If not, lay your difficulties before some friend who is a successful teacher, and get advice. *Anything*, rather than going on, week after week, without improvement. There *is* a way of interesting your class in their lessons, of securing good order and punctual attendance, of making the scholars learn. Only make up your mind that you will find out what that way is. If you think it cannot be done, of course it will not be done. If you have fairly made up your mind that it *may* be done, and that *you* can do it, it is half done already.

You have no idea how much more pleasant the work will be, when you have once learned how to do it. One reason why so many teachers desert the ranks, is the irksomeness produced by want of success. Few things are more intolerable than being obliged to do a thing while conscious of doing it in an awkward and bungling manner. On the other hand, almost any work is a pleasure, which one is conscious of doing well.

XVI.

TEACHING POWER.

TEACHERS differ greatly in their ability to bring a class forward in intellectual acquisition and growth. With one teacher pupils are all life and energy, they take hold of difficulties with courage, their ideas become clear, their very power of comprehension seems to gather strength. With another teacher, those same pupils, studying the same subject, are dull, heavy, easily discouraged, and make almost no progress. The ability thus to stimulate the intellectual activity of others, to give it at once momentum and progress, is the true measure of one's teaching power. It may be well to consider for a moment some of the conditions necessary to the existence and the exercise of this power.

In the first place, we can exert no great, commanding influence over others, whether pupils or not, unless we have in a high degree their confidence. Pupils must have faith in their teacher. I never knew an instance yet, where there was great intellectual ferment going on in a class, that the pupils did not believe the teacher infallible, or very nearly so. This principle of confidence in leadership is one of the great moving powers of the world. In teaching, it is specially important. This feeling may indeed be in excess. It may exist to such an extent as to extinguish all independence of thought, to induce a blind, unquestioning receptivity. Such an extreme is of course opposed to true mental progress. But short of this extreme point, there is almost no amount of faith that children can have in their teacher, that, if well founded, is not of the highest advantage. Seeing the firm, assured tread of father or mother, or of an older brother or sister, is a great aid to the tottering little one in putting forth its own steps while learning to walk. So the child is emboldened to send out its young, unpractised thoughts, by the confidence it has in the guidance and protection of its teacher. To acquire and retain the proper ascendancy over the mind of a child, two things are essential, ample knowledge and entire honesty. Shallowness and pretension may mislead for a while. But to hold a child firmly and permanently, the teacher must abound in knowledge, and must have thoroughly honest convictions.

The next condition to great teaching power is confidence in one's self. A timid, irresolute, hesitating utterance of one's own convictions fails to produce conviction in the minds of others. I do not recommend self-conceit. It is not necessary to be dogmatic. Yet a certain style of self-assertion, bordering very closely upon these qualities, is needed in the teacher. In the higher regions of science and opinion, there are of course many points about which no one, at least no one well informed, would undertake to speak with authority. Such subjects it becomes us all to approach with reverent humility, as at the best only inquirers after truth. But the case is very different with teachers of the common branches concerned in our present remarks. On these points the teacher ought to have a certainty and a readiness of knowledge, so as to be thoroughly self-reliant before the class. Teaching is like fighting. Self-reliance is half the battle.

Equally important with the former is it to have the affection of one's pupils. Writers on metaphysics now-a-days dwell much, and very properly, on the influence of the body upon the mind, and the necessity of a healthy condition of the former in order to the full clearness and strength of our intellectual apprehensions. There is a still more intimate connection between our moral emotions and our mental action. The wish is father to the thought, in more senses than that intended by Shakspeare. If the intellect is the seeing power of the soul, the affections are the atmosphere through which we look. The same object may appear to us very differently, as it is seen through the colorless medium of pure intellectual perception, or as it is enlarged and glorified by the mellowing haze of fond affection, or as it is distorted and obscured by the mists of prejudice and hate. When a child has a thorough dislike for a subject or for his teacher, the difficulty of learning is very greatly increased. Not only is the willingness to study weak or wanting, but the very power of mental perception seems to be obstructed. The power of attention, the power of apprehension, the power of memory, the power of reasoning, are all paralyzed by dislike, and are equally vitalized by love and desire. Mental action, in short, is influenced by the state of the heart as much as by the state of the body. If you do not expect great mental efforts from a child that is sickly, burning with fever, or racked with pain, neither may you expect the best and highest results from one whose heart is diseased and alienated, who approaches a subject with feelings of aversion and dislike, whose conceptions are clouded with prejudice.

A teacher of great intellectual force, and with an overbearing will, may push forward even a reluctant and a rebellious class with a certain degree of speed. On the other hand, a teacher who enjoys the unbounded love of his scholars, may accomplish comparatively little, on account of lacking the other qualities needed for success. The highest measure of success in teaching is attained only where these several conditions meet,—where the teacher has and deserves the full confidence of the scholars, where he has full confidence in himself, is self-reliant and self-asserting, and where at the same time he has the warm affection of his pupils. Love, after all, is the governing power of the human soul, as it is the crowning grace in the Christian scheme. Love is, in teaching, what sunshine and showers are in vegetation. By a system of forcing and artificial culture, the gardener may indeed produce a few hot-house plants, but for all great or general results, he must look to the genial operations of nature.

XVII.

GROWING.

CHILDREN often use the term "grown-up people." By it they mean persons who have come to the age of twenty, or twenty-one, and whose bodily growth is complete. But there are other kinds of growth, besides that of the body.

What is a "grown-up" *teacher?* It is not difficult, certainly, to find some, in every locality, to whom this term could *not* be applied, with any propriety. They have been engaged for years in the work, and yet they are the merest babes. They have no more skill than when they first took a class in hand. When a boy begins to use a penknife, he is very awkward. He cuts himself about as often as he cuts the stick. After a while, however, he learns to manage the matter better. He finds out how to handle the curious instrument with skill and even with elegance. But you will see teachers, so called, who seem never to make any of this progress in their work. They have no more idea now, than they had when they gave their first lesson, of what they must do to secure attention and silence, how they must manage to keep all the children busy, how to secure good attendance, or study of the lesson, how to gain affection and confidence, how to enforce order and obedience, how to do anything, except to sit, book in hand, and ask the questions one after the other round the class, and see that John, George, and James severally say the answers correctly. This is the idea of teaching with which they begin, and they make no progress towards anything better. They acquire no skill. They make no growth. They are "grown-up" bodily. But in all that pertains to teaching, they are still babes. They whittle as awkwardly and unskilfully as when the delicate instrument was first put into their clumsy fingers. They go on from year to year and learn nothing.

Some persons are born teachers, just as some are born poets or mechanics. That is, they are gifted with a natural aptitude for that particular work. But those most gifted by nature, are capable of improvement, and those having least natural gifts for teaching, may acquire a certain and a very considerable amount of skill, by proper observation and study. The point which I wish to make, and which I deem important, is, that teachers should not rest content with their present qualifications, whatever they may be, whether large or small. Let it be the aim of every one to be a growing teacher. We come short, if we are not better teachers this year than we were last. We should aim and resolve to be better teachers next year than we are now. Our education as teachers should never be considered as finished. Forgetting the things which are behind, let us ever press forward. Let us constantly aim upward. Skill in teaching admits of infinite degrees, and no one will ever be perfect in it. Efforts at improvement, if persistently followed up, are always rewarded with success, and success in such a work brings a most sweet recompense. What satisfaction is equal to that of feeling that one is steadily increasing in the power of guiding and moulding the minds of others? Growing skill in anything, even in works requiring mechanical ingenuity, brings joy to the mind. How much more intense and pure the joy, when there is a consciousness of growth in this higher department of mental power?

Will the teacher, who reads these paragraphs, consider the matter? Are you, as a teacher, growing? or are you working on in dull content in the same old routine? On your answer to these questions depend very largely, not only the welfare of your scholars and the amount of good you will achieve, but your own happiness and satisfaction in your work. The artist, who produces some great work of genius, has his reward not merely in the dollars which it may bring to his coffer, but in the inward satisfaction which successful achievement produces. The true artist is always struggling towards some unattainable ideal, and his joy is proportioned to the nearness of his approach to the imagined perfection. So in proportion as we approach in skill the great Teacher, will be our joy in the work itself, apart from our joy in the results.

To be a growing teacher requires a distinct aim to this end, and a resolute and persistent effort. It does not come by chance. It is not a weed that springs up spontaneously, and matures without culture. It is not the fruit of mere wishing. There must be *will*, A DETERMINED AND RESOLUTE WILL. Rules and theories will not accomplish it. There are books and essays in abundance on the art and practice of teaching. But back of means we must have, first of all, the propelling power. Have you made up your mind to be stationary, or have you resolved to go forward? Will you remain in the wilderness, or will you advance into the promised land and take possession? Are you a deliberate, predetermined, contented dwarf, or will you resolutely grow? You may never become a giant, but do not remain an infant.

If there is any one duty of the teacher more imperative than another, it is that of continued, persistent self-improvement. No element of progress is so efficient as a wholesome discontent. "I count not myself to *have* attained," says the great apostle of progress. To sit down self-satisfied with present attainments is in itself a sign that you have not yet risen much. It is to belong to the owls and the bats of the lower valleys. One must already have ascended to lofty heights before he can even see the higher Alps towering beyond.

The teacher who would improve must, in a good sense, be restless. He must bestir himself. He must study and read and experiment, attend teachers' meetings and conventions, and take teachers' papers, and find out what other teachers are doing and have done, ever remembering that improvement comes mainly by comparison.

XVIII.

LOVING THE CHILDREN.

SOME teachers make the mistake of supposing that a love for the work and a love for the children are one and the same thing. The two things are certainly separable in thought, and they are often actually separated in action. It is of some importance to teachers to remember the difference.

We see persons every day struggling with all their might to accomplish certain results. They have certain ideas which they wish to realize, certain theories which they wish to verify. To bring about these results, is a matter of pride with them. So that the end is gained, the means to be used are a matter of comparative indifference. Their heart is set on the result, they care nothing for the machinery by which it is brought about. Now, so long as the work is of a nature which requires only the use of mechanical powers, or of mere brute force, it is all very well. The sculptor need not fall in love with the block of marble on which he is working, in order to realize from it the conception of his mind. The engine which carries us thirty miles an hour towards the goal of our desires, will not speed us more or less for not being an object of our affections. But every man has a natural and proper dislike to becoming a mere machine for carrying out the schemes of others. Children especially revolt at being treated in this way. If a teacher takes the charge of a class or of a school, for the purpose of showing to himself or to others how certain things may be done, the children are quick to find it out, and to resent it. No child, however humble or obscure, but feels indignant at being considered as a mere pawn upon a chess-board, or a mere wheel or pulley in some complicated piece of machinery. Every individual child is to itself the centre of all human interests, and if you are to have any real and abiding influence upon him, he must first feel that you have a regard for himself, in his own proper person, independently of any schemes or plans of your own.

You may love to see your children all present punctually, to see them making a good appearance, and by their orderly behavior and manners helping forward the school generally; you may love the work of teaching as giving you honorable and useful occupation. But something more than this is wanting. *You must love the children.* You must love each particular child. You must become interested in each child, not for what it is to you, or to the class, or to the school, but for what it is in itself, as a precious jewel, to be loved and admired, for those immortal qualities and capacities which belong to it as a human being. No matter how degraded or depraved or forbidding in appearance that child may be, it has qualities which, if brought out, may make it more glorious than an angel. If Jesus loved him, you may love him. Jesus did not stand off at a distance from the loathsome and filthy leper, while performing the miracle of healing. He first "*touched*" the leper, and said, "Be thou clean." We are sometimes too fastidious in our benevolence, and shrink too much from coming into contact with those whom we would befriend.

Little real influence is ever produced upon any human being, without creating between you and him a bond of sympathy. If we would work strongly and efficiently upon the minds of children, we must really love them, not in the abstract, not in a general way, but concretely and individually. We must love John and William and Mary and Susie, simply and purely because he or she is, in himself or herself alone, an object of true interest and affection. In looking over a school, it is not difficult to discover at a glance which teachers thus love their children. It speaks in every word from the lips. It beams in every look from the eyes. It thrills in every tone of the voice. It has a language in the very touch of the hand and the movements of the person.

Some persons are naturally more fond of children than others are. But those not naturally thus inclined may cultivate the disposition. They *must* do so if they mean to be teachers. No one is fitted to be a teacher, who has not learned to sympathize with the real wants and feelings of children. Pretence here is all wasted. Shams may do with grown persons sometimes, never with children. They have an instinctive perception of what is genuine and what is pretended, in professed love for them. In fact, the way to win the affection of a child is to love him, not to make professions of love.

It is not always the easiest thing in the world to exercise this love. A teacher may have the charge of a class of children whose appearance, manners, and dispositions are exceedingly forbidding, perhaps even loathsome. Yet observation and study will ordinarily discover some good quality even in the worst and most degraded. A talent for discovering what is good in a child is much more important in the work of elevating him, than the smartness at detecting and exposing his tricks, in which some teachers take pride. It is a bad sign, though not an uncommon one, to see evidences of cunning in a teacher. Better by far to be outwitted and duped occasionally, than to forfeit that character of perfect sincerity and straightforwardness which secures the confidence of a child. The teacher who would love his children, particularly if he happens to have been entrusted with an unpromising class, must learn to wear the spectacles of charity. He must cultivate the habit of seeing things in their best light. While not blind to faults, he must be prompt and eagle-eyed to spy out every indication of good. Above all, he must remember that no human soul, however degraded, is without some elements and possibilities of good, for whom there is the possibility that Christ died.

XIX.

GAINING THE AFFECTIONS OF THE SCHOLARS.

THE importance of this point is not to be measured by the mere gratification it affords. It adds undoubtedly to the happiness of the teacher in his work, to know that his scholars love him. Nor is this a small consideration. The teacher has many vexatious rubs. He encounters much toil and self-denial; and whatever tends to mitigate these asperities, and to make his labor sweet, is for that very reason important. The teacher has, for a part at least of his reward, the enjoyment of a love as pure and unselfish as any known upon earth. He will doubtless go forward in duty, even where he fails of obtaining this precious foretaste of the heavenly bliss, and he has doubtless higher aims than any arising from mere gratification, of whatever sort. Yet a boon so great is not to be despised or ignored. The ardent love which scholars sometimes give to their teachers is a high gratification, and something to be greatly prized for the mere pleasure it gives.

And yet, after all, this is not its main value. The fact that children love their teacher, gives to the teacher almost unbounded influence over them. There is hardly a point, necessary to the success of a school or of a class, that

scholars will not readily yield to a teacher whom they love. By this silken cord they can be drawn whithersoever the teacher wills. To please teacher, they will attend regularly, will come punctually, will be quiet and orderly, will learn their lessons, will be attentive to instruction. More than all this, many a child, by the love of an earthly friend, has been led to the love of his heavenly Friend. The young heart is opened to receive the Saviour, by the warmth of its love for one who so manifestly bears his image. Perhaps there is no one, not even excepting a mother, who can so easily bring the young to the Saviour, as the teacher who has thoroughly succeeded in winning his scholars' affections.

There is another consideration in this matter, not so weighty as the one named, yet of great importance, and the more worthy to be named, because it is generally not rightly understood. I refer to the fact that children will learn so much more readily under a teacher whom they love. Not only will they study better, and be more attentive, for the sake of pleasing their teacher, but by some mysterious process of the mind, love helps us to understand, as dislike disturbs and beclouds the understanding. When a child has a dislike or prejudice or ill-feeling of any kind against a teacher, or a subject of study, the effect upon the mind of the child is like that produced upon a spring of pure and sparkling water by stirring up the mud and sediment from the bottom. In the human organization the heart is at the bottom, and disturbing influences there cause us to see things through an impure medium. The calmness and serenity, produced by perfect love and

trust, are the proper conditions for the right and best working of the understanding. We must get the heart right if we would see truth clearly, and that teacher who has won the love of his scholars has done much towards making the path of knowledge easy for them.

Let the teacher, then, aim to win the love of his scholars, first, because this love is in itself a boon to which the teacher has a rightful claim; secondly, because it gives him a powerful influence in moulding the character and habits of the children, and especially in bringing them to the Saviour; and, thirdly, because it helps the scholars intellectually, enabling them to understand better and to learn faster.

But how is this love to be gained?

Assuredly, *not* by demanding it as a right, or by fretting, complaining, or scolding because your scholars do not love you. Love only is the price for love. If you wish your scholars to love you, you must first love them, not pretend to do it,—children are quick to see through such pretences,—but really and truly love them.

Many teachers, however, sincerely love their scholars, and yet do not succeed in winning their affections. Something in their manner and appearance is repulsive. There is in the face of some good people a hard and forbidding look, at which the heart takes alarm and retires within itself. The young heart, like the young buds in springtime, requires an atmosphere of warmth and sunshine. If we would draw forth their warm affections towards us, we must not only feel love towards them in our hearts, but we must wear sunshine in our faces. A pleasant smile, a loving word, a soft, endearing tone of the voice, goes a great way with a child, especially where it is not put on, but springs from a loving heart.

Some teachers in avoiding this hard, repulsive manner, run to the opposite extreme, and lose the respect of their scholars by undue familiarity. Children do not expect you to become their playmate and fellow, before giving you their love and confidence. Their native tendency is to look up. They yearn for repose upon one superior to themselves. Only, when the tender heart of youth thus looks up, let it not be into a region filled with clouds and cold, but into a sky everywhere pervaded with a clear, steady, warm sunlight. Let there be no frown upon your brow, no harsh or angry word upon your lips, no exacting sternness in your eye. Let the love which you feel in your heart beam forth naturally and spontaneously in loving looks and words, and you need not fear but that you will meet with a response.

XX.

THE OBEDIENCE OF CHILDREN.

THERE is much misapprehension as to the true nature of obedience. Wherein does obedience really consist? What is its essence?

Merely doing a specified act, which has been required, is not necessarily an act of obedience. A father may have a rule of his household that the children shall rise in the morning at five o'clock. A son who habitually disregards this rule, may rise at the appointed time on a particular morning, in order to join a companion on a fishing excursion, or for some object connected solely with his own pleasure and convenience. Here the external act is the one required. He rises at the hour enjoined by his father's command. But his doing so has no reference to his father's wishes. It is not in any sense an act of obedience. Something more than mere external compliance with a rule or a command is needed to constitute obedience. In other words, not only the act itself must be the one required, but the motive must be right.

If I am led to do what my father or my mother requires, by mere dint of coaxing, or by the expectation of cakes or pennies or promised indulgence of any kind, if it is a bargain, in which I give so much compliance for so much per contra of self-gratification, the compliance rendered is not an act of obedience. As well might a man profess to obey his neighbor, because he gives him a bag of oats for a bag of corn. A great deal of what passes for obedience in families and schools, is mere barter. Strip the matter of all glosses and disguises, and the naked truth remains, that children are hired to do what the parent or the teacher wants to have done. They do not obey, in any legitimate and wholesome use of the word. They are quiet when they should be quiet, they learn the lessons which they should learn, they abstain from whatever things they should abstain from, because they have learned that this is the only way to gain the indulgences which they desire. The parent and the teacher use a motive adequate to secure the outward act, but they do not secure obedience.

It is not obedience for a child to do a thing because his reason and conscience tell him that the act in itself, without reference to his parents' wishes, is right and proper. At least it is not filial obedience. I may be obeying my conscience, but I am not obeying my father. Many parents, who are above the weakness of bribing their children, satisfy themselves by reasoning with them. Far be it from us to say a word against any legitimate appeal to the reason and conscience of a child. Children, at the proper age, should be taught to reason and to judge for themselves, in regard to the right and wrong of actions, just as they should learn to walk alone, and not be forever dependent upon leading strings. Only, let it be understood that just so far as the child acts on its own independent judgment, the act is not one of filial obedience.

Obedience is doing a thing because another, having competent authority, has enjoined it. The motive necessary to constitute any act an act of obedience, is a reference to the will and authority of another. It is submission of our will to the will of another. The child receives as true what his parents say, and because they say it; so, he does as right what they command, and because they command it. That fact is, and in the first instance it should be, to the child's mind, the ultimate and sufficient reason for either believing or doing — for faith or obedience. This faith and obedience rendered to my earthly father, which is only partial and temporary, besides serving its own immediate ends, in securing a well-ordered household and my own best interests as a child, has the further end of training me for that unqualified faith and obedience, which I am to render to my heavenly Father, and which is of universal and permanent obligation. One object of the parental relation seems to be to fit the soul for this higher obedience. I must, however, learn to obey my father simply because he is my father, and because as such he has the right to command me, if thereby I am to learn, for a like reason, to obey my heavenly Father. No lower motive will secure the end.

Submission to parental authority is not always the instinctive impulse of childhood. Where this submission is not yielded, it must be enforced. Authority, in other words, requires sanctions. The father has no right to command, unless he has the right to punish in case of disobedience. Furthermore, if he does not, especially in the early childhood of his offspring, train them to a habit of real obedience and submission to authority, he does his children a great wrong. He deprives them of the benefit of that habit of obedience, which will be of the utmost value to them in their future religious life.

A man forbids his child to eat green apples. The child abstains. That abstinence is not necessarily an act of obedience.

He may abstain because his mother offers, in case of his doing so, to give him sugar-plums, and he prefers the sugar-plums to the apples. This is not obedience.

Or, his reason and experience may have taught him that the eating of green fruit will cause him sickness and pain, and so he abstains for the same reasons that his father, mother, or anybody else does. This is not obedience.

But children often have not the forethought to look at remote consequences, or they have not the strength of purpose to deny a present gratification for the sake of a distant good, and especially for a good of which they have only a vague idea through the representations of their parents or teachers. Suppose such a case. Suppose a child with a strong inclination and desire for the thing forbidden, and with no clear apprehension that there is anything wrong or hurtful in the indulgence, except in the fact that the father has forbidden it, and with no temptation of a higher indulgence as a reward for abstaining. If, in such a case, the child abstains, he performs a true act of obedience. He really subjects his will to the will of his father.

This kind of implicit obedience is greatly needed. It is to be secured just as our heavenly Father secures obedience to some of his laws. If a child thrusts his finger into the candle, he violates a law, and he instantly suffers for it. We are surrounded by many such laws, without the observance of which we could not live a day. To teach us obedience to these laws, the penalty of transgression is immediate and sharp. There are other laws of our physical well-being, the penalties of which are remote, and in regard to those we have room for the exercise and cultivation of our reasoning powers. Now in childhood, there are many things which a child should be taught to forbear doing as promptly as he forbears to thrust his hand into the fire. Yet for these things there is no natural penalty. Here the command of the parent should be interposed, and transgression should be promptly followed by penalty. The authority of the parent and the penalties by which he sustains it, guide the child during those years when reason and the power of self-denial are weak. But to make this discipline easy and effective, there should be no hesitation or uncertainty about the exercise of it. Parents often have to strain their authority, and use very largely their right of punishment, because they are so unequal and irregular in their methods of government. A child soon ceases to thrust his finger into the fire. Fire is not a thing which burns one day, and may be safely tampered with the next. So, if disobedience, invariably and promptly, without passion or caprice, and with the uniformity of a law of nature, brings such a penalty as to make the disobedience painful, there will be little transgression and little need of punishment. A child does not fret because he cannot play with fire. He will not fret because he cannot transgress a father's direct command, if he once knows that such commands *must* be obeyed.

XXI.

RAREY AS AN EDUCATOR.

PARENTS, teachers, and all who are charged with the duty of training the young, may learn important lessons from the example of the late Mr. Rarey. The principles on which the horse is rendered obedient and docile do not differ essentially from those to be employed in the government of children or of men.

Some of the accounts of Mr. Rarey's system, however, which have been published, are liable to mislead, and to foster a mischievous error. His procedure was eminently kind and gentle. The horse became fully assured that no harm was intended towards him. This conviction is essential to success in securing a perfect and willing obedience, whether from brute or human. But the distinctness with which this feature of the treatment was brought out in Mr. Rarey's exhibitions, led some apparently to think that this was the main, if not the only feature. Kindness alone, however, will not tame, and will not govern, brutes or men. There must be power. There must be, in the mind of the party to be governed, a full conviction that the power of the other party is superior to his own — that there is, in the party claiming obedience, an ample reserve of power fully adequate to enforce the claim. The more complete this conviction is, the less occasion there will be for the exercise of the power. The most headstrong horse, once convinced that he is helpless in this contest of strength, and convinced at the same time that his master is his friend, may be led by a straw.

Mr. Rarey went through various preliminary steps, the object of which was to make the horse acquainted with him, and to prevent fright or panic. But obedience was not claimed, and was not given, until there had been a demonstration of power — until the horse was convinced that the man was entirely too much for him. By a very simple adjustment of straps to the forefeet of the animal, he became perfectly helpless in the hands of his tamer. The struggle, indeed, was sometimes continued for a good while. The horse put forth his prodigious strength to the utmost. He became almost wild at the perfect ease and quietude with which all his efforts were baffled, until at length, fully satisfied that further struggles were useless, he made a complete surrender, and lay down as peaceful and submissive as an infant.

This point is of some importance. I do not underrate the value of kindness and love in any system of government, whether in the household, the school, the stable, the menagerie, or in civil society. But love is not the basis of government. Obedience is yielded to authority, and authority is based on right and power. The child who complies with his father's wishes, only because a different course would make his father grieve, or give his mother a headache, or because his parents have reasoned with him and shown him that compliance is for his good, or who has been wheedled into compliance by petty bribes and promises, has not learned that doctrine of obedience which lies at the foundation of all government, human and divine. God has given to the parent the right to the obedience of his children, and the power to enforce it. That parent has failed in his duty who has not trained his child, not only to love him, but to obey him, in the strict sense of the word, that is to yield his will to the will of a superior, from a sense of appointed subordination and rightful authority. This sense of subordination and of obedience to appointed and rightful authority, is of the very essence of civil government, and the place where it is to be first and chiefly learned is in the household. To teach this is a main end of the parental relation. The parent who fails to teach it, fails to give his child the first element of good citizenship, and leaves him often to be in after-years the victim of his own uncontrolled passions and tempers. The want of a proper exercise of parental authority is, in this age of the world, the most prolific source of those frightful disorders that pervade society, and that threaten to upturn the very foundations of all civil government. The feeling of reverence, the sense of a respect for authority, the consciousness of being in a state of subordination, the feeling of obligation to do a thing simply because it is commanded by some one having a right to obedience — all these old-fashioned notions seem to be dying out of the minds of men. The popular cry is, Don't make your children fear you. Govern them by love. Conquer them by kindness. Treat them as Mr Rarey did his horses.

I protest against the notion. It is a mistake of Mr.

Rarey's system, and it is not the true basis for government, whether of brutes or men. The doctrine may seem harsh in these dainty times. But, in my opinion, a certain degree of wholesome fear in the mind of a child towards its parent, is essential, and is perfectly compatible with the very highest love. I have never known more confiding, affectionate, and loving children, than those who not only regarded their parents as kind benefactors and sympathizing friends, but who looked up to them with a certain degree of reverence. The fear spoken of in the Bible, as being cast out by perfect love, is quite a different emotion. It is rather a slavish fear, a feeling of dread and terror. It sees in its object not only power but hostility. It awakens not only dread but hate. The child's fear, on the contrary, sees power united with kindness. It obeys the one, it loves the other. It is the exact attitude of mind to which Mr. Rarey brought the horse that was subjected to his management.

XXII.

A BOARDING-SCHOOL EXPERIENCE.

I HAVE often wished I had the descriptive power of the man who wrote "The Diary of a Physician." My experiences in another profession have not been wanting in incident, often of a curious and romantic kind, and sometimes almost startling. But the "Diary of a Schoolmaster," to be read with interest, requires something more than a good basis of facts. He who writes it must have, also, graphic and narrative powers — a special gift, of which nature has been sparing to me. I had one experience, however, many years ago, so remarkable in some of its features, that perhaps the bare facts, stated in the simplest form, without artifice or embellishment, will be found worthy of perusal. The youth who was the principal actor in the scene which I am about to describe, has been dead these many years, and I believe the family have nearly all died out. The only survivor that I knew anything of ten years ago was then blind, and ill of an incurable disease. There would, therefore, perhaps be no harm in giving the youth's real name; but as the name is one widely known, and as it is always best to avoid unnecessary intrusion upon private affairs, I have concluded to use a fictitious name, both for the person referred to and for the place from which he came. In other particulars the following incident is a simple narration of facts.

At the time of which I am writing, I had a large boarding-school for boys, at Princeton, New Jersey. Particular circumstances gave me, for several years, quite a run of patronage from a town in one of the Western States, which for convenience I shall call Tompkinsville. Among those who applied for admission from this town were two brothers, Bob and Charlie Graham. Bob was only ten years old. Charlie was fourteen, and as mature as most boys at nineteen. Mature, I mean, not so much in his intellectual development, for in that respect he was rather behindhand, but in his passions, and in his habits of independent thought and action.

I had many misgivings about the propriety of receiving these boys into the school. Most of those that I had already from Tompkinsville were of the fire-eating class, whom it had taken all my skill as a disciplinarian to bring into subjection, and I did not know what might be the effect of adding to their number two such combustible youths as these Grahams were reputed to be. Tompkinsville, indeed, had long been notorious for the fiery and lawless character of its inhabitants. While containing many most estimable families, where a generous and warm-hearted hospitality reigned supreme, yet no town, probably, in all the Western States witnessed annually a greater number of street-fights and other deeds of violence of the most desperate character. No family in Tompkinsville were more noted than the Grahams, on the one hand for the passionate warmth of their attachments, and on the other for the fierceness and violence of their resentments. Nothing was too much for them to do for you when their affections were touched. On the other hand, no law, human or divine, seemed to restrain them when their blood was up. When roused by what they regarded as an insult, they were human tigers, no less in the quickness than in the desperate ferocity of their anger. The father once, in open court, in a sudden rage, actually strode over the tables and heads of the lawyers, and seizing the presiding judge by the collar, dragged him from the bench and horsewhipped him in the presence of all his officials. Charlie himself, of whom I am writing, gave, about two years after leaving school, a similar demonstration of violence. Hearing that a young man, who was a fellow-student of his in a law office, had done something insulting, Charlie drew up a formal written apology and presented it to the young man to sign, intending afterwards to post it. On the young man's refusing to sign the paper, Charlie drew a weapon of some kind and sprang upon him. The young man being several years older, and very large and powerful, had no difficulty in disarming his assailant, throwing him upon the floor and holding him there. While thus down upon his back, bound hand and foot, and completely at the mercy of his antagonist, Charlie still demanded, as fiercely as ever, the signing of the "apology," giving the young man, as the only alternative, either to kill him or to be killed. "If you let me up alive, I will shoot you at sight, as sure as my name is Charles Graham." Knowing the desperate character of the family, and feeling too well assured of his own social position to care for any effect the signing of such a paper might have, the young man courageously let the ruffian up and signed the apology. Two days after, Charlie came back to the office, thoroughly mortified and penitent for his outrage, voluntarily gave up the paper, and apologized in the amplest manner for his folly.

I might enumerate other instances by the score, were it necessary, to show the character of the boy with whom I had to deal. But these are probably sufficient. His passions were as quick as gunpowder, and as indiscriminate. Had I known all that I afterwards knew in regard to his disposition and his antecedents, I certainly would not have undertaken the charge of his education.

The Grahams had been with me nearly a year without the occurrence of anything to attract attention or call for discipline. The school had considerable reputation among the people of Tompkinsville for the strictness of its discipline. Though the relations between the pupils and myself were for the most part thoroughly kind and friendly, yet it was well understood by every boy who entered school that the will of the Principal was supreme. Mr. Graham had probably brought his boys to the school for that very reason. The routine of obedience had been so thoroughly established, that his boys, he thought, would submit through mere force of example. Bob was too young to give any uneasiness. He fell, of course, into many of the peccadilloes of boys of his age, and received, without demur, the treatment of a little boy. Charlie, for a long time, was almost a model of propriety. He was diligent in his studies, and observed the rules of the school with scrupulous care. He was fair, almost girlish, in appearance, and gentle in his speech. No one, merely observing the quiet, modest boy, going about his usual routine of duty, without noise or turbulence, would have dreamed of the sleeping volcano that lay beneath this placid exterior.

About the middle of the second term I began to notice in Charlie symptoms that I did not like. The harness evidently chafed him somewhere, and there was no telling when he might kick out of the traces. The crisis at length came. One morning, when the boys were in the wash-room, under the charge of the senior teacher, Charlie, with what precise provocation I could never ascertain, drew back his basin of water and threw it full into the teacher's face.

Here was a case. We were about to have an explosion. Evidently the young fire-eater's blood was up. He was bent on having "a scene;" and, while his hand was in, he would quite likely make up for all the long months of peaceful inaction. All the tiger within him stood revealed.

The matter was reported to me of course. After some little thought, my plan was chosen. Not a word was said on the subject for several hours. Meals, play-time, study-hours, lessons, everything went on as usual. At length, about eleven o'clock, Charlie was summoned, not to the principal's desk, in the public school-room, but to my private office, in a remote part of the premises. As he entered the quiet apartment, it was evident that the intervening hours of reflection had not been lost upon him. He was pretty sure, of course, that I had sent for him in consequence of the occurrence of the morning. Still he was not certain. Not a word had been uttered in school on the subject — no allusion to it even. Altogether there was something about the affair that mystified him.

The following brief dialogue ensued.

"Where are your skates, Charlie?"

"In my box in the play-room, sir."

"Where is your sled?"

"That is hanging up in the outer shed."

"Where is your fishing-line and your ball?"

"They are in the play-room."

"I wish you would get these and all your other play-things together before dinner. Peter (this was the head waiter) has collected your boots and shoes, and Sarah (the seamstress) has got your clothes together and packed your trunks. I have made out your accounts, and will be ready to send you home to your father by the afternoon train. You may help Bob also to collect his playthings; he has not done anything wrong, but he is so young I think your father would not like to have him here alone so far from home."

All this was said in a tone as utterly emotionless as I would have used if asking him whether he would be helped to beef or lamb at table.

Charlie was taken aback. If I had attempted to chastise him, if I had even used towards him the language of invective or reproach, he could have met the case. But here was an issue which he had never contemplated. After a moment of blank amazement, he said:

"Mr. H., I don't want to go home thus. It will grieve

my father, and it will be a lasting stigma to me in Tompkinsville, where it is counted an honor to belong to this school. I know I have done wrong, but can't you inflict some other punishment? I will submit to anything rather than be sent home in this way. Put me in 'exile' and at the 'side-table,' for three days, or any time you please!"

This was an extreme penalty, sometimes used in school for very grave offences. The boy who was subject to it was obliged to stand at a table by himself in the dining-room and eat bread and water, while the other boys and their teachers were at their meals. Besides this, during the continuance of the penalty the culprit was not allowed to go upon the play-ground, or to speak to any one, nor was any one allowed to speak to him, under the penalty of being himself similarly punished. The punishment was, of course, a severe one in itself, and was very mortifying to a boy of high spirit. It was only resorted to in extreme cases, and was limited to one day. Charlie begged that I would "exile" and "side-table" him for a week, if I pleased; only not send him home thus.

"No, Charlie; I am not sure that your father would approve of your being thus publicly disgraced before the school and the family, nor am I myself sure that it would be right in the case of a boy so far advanced towards manhood as you are. In assuming the charge of you, I never contemplated anything in our intercourse but such as occurs between gentlemen. Since I have been mistaken in my estimate of you, let our intercourse cease. It would not alter your character to subject you to a humiliating punishment before the assembled school. If it were your brother Bob, the case would be different. But you are almost a man. You have been treated here, as at home, with the consideration due to a young gentleman. I would myself revolt at seeing one of your years and standing treated as you request me to treat you. I cannot do it. You must go home."

"Oh, no! no! Do not send me home! Do anything else. I will submit to any punishment you please. Flog me; *please*, flog me!"

"Flog you! Never! I have no scruples, as you know, on the subject of corporal punishment, for I often chastise the smaller boys; but boys as old and mature as you are have sense enough to be governed by other considerations than fear, and especially fear of the rod. If they have not, I want nothing to do with them."

"Oh! Mr. H., won't you *please* to flog me?"

And the boy actually went down on his knees and begged me to thrash him. He, Charlie Graham, whose veins ran fire, who, six hours before, would have leaped at my throat had I so much as raised my finger at him, was now begging me, as a special boon, to give him a whipping! I could hardly believe my senses. Yet there was no doubt of the boy's sincerity, or of his earnestness. So, to give me time to reflect as to what should be done, I finally said, "Charlie, I will think of what you have asked, and let you know at three o'clock."

Three o'clock came, and Charlie again made his appearance.

"Do you still wish me to whip you?"

"I do. I will make any apology you think proper to

the teacher whom I insulted, and I will be most thankful to you to chastise me for the offence."

"Please to take off your coat."

* * * * * * * * *

When the painful affair was over, I gave him my hand cordially and frankly, and said, "Charlie, you have honorably and courageously atoned for a grievous fault, and I assure you, I restore you not only to your position in school, but to my respect and confidence."

I never had any further difficulty with Charlie Graham. Years afterwards, when I met his father at the Springs, he could hardly contain his amazement when I told him that I had once flogged his oldest son Charlie, at his own particular request. It was, I suppose, the first and last time the hand of correction was ever laid on him.

XXIII.

PHRENOLOGY.

IN the previous chapter I gave a leaf from my experience of life in a boarding-school. I propose now to give another leaf from the same book. The incident about to be narrated, however, is not given as an illustration of boarding-school life, but merely because it happened at school. It might have happened elsewhere, though the circumstances on that occasion were particularly favorable for giving to it a curious point.

While I was at the head of the Edgehill school, at Princeton, N. J., a stranger called one day and announced himself as Prof. ——. The name is one almost as well known in the history of Phrenological science as that of Prof. Combe. He said he was about to give a lecture in Princeton on the subject of Phrenology, and as he was an entire stranger to myself and to all the pupils and teachers in the school, he thought it would be a good opportunity for making an interesting and critical experiment. He proposed, therefore, with my consent, to spend an hour, in presence of the school, in examining the heads of any of the boys that I might call up for that purpose. From the very intimate relations existing in a boarding-school, the characters of the boys would be well known to me and to their companions and teachers, and we would have therefore the means of knowing how far he succeeded in his experiment.

Thinking that an hour spent in this way would not be misspent, that it would at least give some variety to the monotonous routine of study and lessons, and, let me add, being not entirely without curiosity as to the result, I consented to his proposition, and called the school together in the large assembly-room. All the boys being in their seats, together with the teachers and the ladies of the household, I stated briefly the object of their assembling and the method in which it was proposed to proceed with the experiment. They were to observe entire silence, and to give no indication, by word or look, so far as they could help it, to show whether the Professor was hitting the mark or not, as he read off to them the characters of their companions. The boys took to the idea at once, and the excitement very soon was at fever-heat.

Placing a chair upon the platform, in full view of the school, and the Professor alongside of it, I called up

Boy No. 1.—This happened to be a lad about fourteen, from the interior of Alabama. He was the most athletic boy in school. "Full big he was of brawn and eke of bones," as Chaucer says, in his picture of the Miller. He could beat any boy in school in wrestling, and no doubt could flog any of them in a fist-fight, though on this point I speak only from conjecture, as this part of boys' amusements is not always as well known to their teachers as it is to the boys themselves. The Professor, after some little manipulation of the cranium, read off the boy's character with tolerable accuracy. Any one, however, with a grain of observation, who had seen the boy stalking up to the platform, with bold, almost defiant air, or had noticed his bull-neck, hard fist, and swaggering gait, could not have had much difficulty in guessing what kind of a boy he was, without resort to his bumps for information. It was written in unmistakable characters all over his physical conformation, from his head to his heels.

I noticed, however, that while the Professor's fingers were busy with the boy's cranium, his eyes were not less busy with the faces of his youthful auditors. Whenever his interpretation of any bump was a palpable hit, his success could be all too plainly read in the upturned faces before him. If the success was very marked and decisive, the youngsters were entirely unable to restrain their expressions of surprise and admiration. It was very evident, from his method of procedure, that he was guided by these expressions, quite as much as by his fingering of the bumps. He would first mention lightly some trait of character. If it attracted no particular attention, he would quietly fall on to something else. But if the announcement seemed to create a little breeze, showing that he had made a hit, he would then dwell upon the point, and intensify his expressions, until, in some instances, the school was in quite an uproar of satisfaction.

Possibly there was a spice of malice in what followed. At all events, it seemed to me that that was a kind of game at which two could play, and if, under the circumstances, he chose to palm off for knowledge gained by the fingers, what he was really getting by means of his eyes and ears, there would be no great crime in punishing him a little for his impertinence. So, in calling the following boys, I selected some who were notorious in school for certain marked traits, but whose general appearance and manner gave no indication of their mental peculiarities; and I questioned the Professor, in regard to each boy, after a method suited to the case.

Boy No. 2 was a youth of moderate abilities, and was, in all things, save one, just like other boys. But, in one matter, he had a peculiarity about which there could be no mistake. That was in the matter of music. So, after questioning the Professor about various indifferent points, moral and intellectual, such as reverence, combativeness, secretiveness, language, ideality, etc., I asked incidentally something also about tune and music. The answer was such as might be safely given in regard to ninety-nine out of every hundred persons — some vague, indefinite epithet that would apply to almost any one. But, seeing a little sparkle in the eyes before him, the gentleman manipulated the cranium again, and then expressed himself somewhat more strongly. As his expressions increased in strength, the excitement of the audience increased, until he was quite lost in hyperbole, as they were in uproar. He even went into particulars. "Now," said he, "though I never saw this boy before, yet I venture to say that his ear for music is so quick that he can pick up almost any tune by once hearing it played or whistled in the street." [A general rustle through the school, boys winking and giving knowing looks one to another.] I dare say he could now sing or whistle a hundred tunes from memory.

[More knowing looks.] Possibly he may never make a very accurate performer, on account of the very ease with which he picks up a tune. He learns a tune so easily by the ear, that he will not submit to the drudgery of studying it scientifically."

"You think, then, Professor, that the boy has decided indications of musical talent?"

"Undoubtedly. He has musical talents of a very high order [suppressed shouts] amounting almost to genius!"

The fact was, poor Charlie was the butt of the whole school, on account of his utter inability to learn the first elements of either the art or the science of music. He could neither sing, whistle, nor play. He could hardly tell "Old Hundred" from "Yankee Doodle." Although he had been taking music-lessons for two years, he could not rise and fall through the eight notes, to save his neck. His attempts to do so were a sort of indiscriminate goo, goo, goo, like that of an infant; and the excitement among the boys, which the Professor had mistaken for applause and admiration, grew out of their astonishment. They were simply laughing at him.

Boy No. 3 was a youth over fourteen years old, regularly and symmetrically formed in face, features, and person. There was nothing in his make or bearing to indicate any marked peculiarity. Yet he had a peculiarity as marked as that of the preceding. He was singularly deficient in the capacity for mathematical studies. He was studying English grammar, geography, and Latin, and got along in these branches about as well as the majority of his class. But when it came to the science of numbers, he seemed to stick fast. Neither I nor any of my teachers had been able to get him beyond Long Division. It was as clear a case as I have ever known of natural deficiency in that department of the mental constitution. Yet this boy was declared by the manipulator to have a decided talent for mathematics.

Boy No. 4 was my crack mathematician. He was really in mathematics what our manipulator had made out No. 2 to be in music. His quickness in the perception of mathematical truth was wonderful. Besides this natural readiness in everything pertaining to the science of quantity and the relations of numbers, he had received a good mathematical training, and he was in this department far in advance of his years. Whenever we had a public exhibition, George was our show-card. The rapidity with which he would fill the blackboard, in solving difficult problems in quadratics, was almost bewildering. It was not every teacher even that could follow him in his quick but exact evolutions of complex algebraical formulæ. In Greek and Latin he hardly attained to mediocrity, being always behind his class, while in mathematics he was superior, not only to every boy in school, but to any boy of the same age that I have ever had in any school. But this boy received from the Professor only a second or third-rate rank for mathematical indications, while highly praised for linguistics, in which he was decidedly inferior.

The fact was, I saw that the gentleman was trying to read *me*, as well as the more youthful part of his audience; and so, in questioning him about this boy, I was malicious enough to be very minute and specific in my inquiries about any indications of a talent for language, while the questions about mathematics were propounded just like those about half a dozen other points; that is, with no special stress or emphasis, but just enough to draw from the Professor a clear and distinct expression of opinion.

Boy No. 5 was perhaps the most critical case of all, yet the one most difficult to describe. He was good, and about equally good, in all his studies. He stood head in almost every class. He was so uniformly good that his character became monotonous, and would have been insipid, but for the manly vigor that marked all his performances. His moral were like his mental traits. He was indeed our model boy. In two years he had not had one demerit mark. He was on all sides rounded and complete — *totus teres atque rotundus.* The uniformity of his goodness was sometimes a source of anxiety to me. There was danger of his growing up with a self-satisfied, pharisaical spirit.

Thus far, however, I have not named the feature which I regarded as the critical one, and which had led me to select him as one of the subjects for examination. Model boys are to be found in all schools. But this boy had a power of reticence which was to me a continual study, and it was this feature in his character that I wanted to bring out in the examination. He was not a sneak. There was nothing sly about him. His conduct was open and aboveboard. What he did was patent to all. But what he thought, or how he felt, no one knew. Not Grant himself could more perfectly keep his own counsel. If a new rule was promulgated, Joseph obeyed it to the letter. But whether it was agreeable or disagreeable to him, no teacher could ever find out. Nor was his obedience of that tame, passive sort which comes from indifference and lack of spirit. We all knew him to be resolute, and to be possessed of strong passions. But his power of self-restraint was equal to his power of reticence. He had, indeed, in a very marked degree, qualities which you look for only in those who have had a long schooling in the stern realities of life, and which you find rarely even then. He was as self-poised as a man of fifty, with not a particle of that easy impulsiveness so nearly universal at his age.

None of the gentleman's performances surprised me so much as the character which he assigned to this boy, and all the more because something of the boy's self-continence and reserve was written upon his face and manner. He was represented by the Professor, in general terms, as having a free and easy, rollicking sort of disposition — not being really worse than his companions, though probably having the reputation of being so. 'If he got into more scrapes than the others [Joseph was never in a scrape in his life], it was more owing to his natural impulsiveness than to anything inherently bad in him. And then, when he did get into a scrape, he had no faculty for concealing it. His organ of secretiveness was unusually small. The boys would hardly admit him to a partnership in their plans of mischief, so sure was he inadvertently to let the cat out of the bag,' etc., etc.

Boy No. 6 was the weakest boy, mentally, that we had in school. He was barely able to take care of himself. Some of his mistakes and blunders were so ridiculous, that they were handed down among the traditionary jokes of the school, and I am afraid even at this day to repeat them, lest they may be recognized. If the manipulator had had the cranium of Daniel Webster under his fingers, he could not have drawn a mental character more marked by every trait that belongs to intellectual greatness of the highest order. Finding that he was making a decided impression upon his young hearers, the Professor continued to pile up qualities and powers, until the scene became almost too much for the most practised gravity.

The examinations occupied an hour, and I made copious notes of the whole, writing down, as nearly as I could, the exact expressions used by the operator. The report which I have now given of it is as nearly literal as it is safe to make it.

When the Professor was through, and was about to leave, he asked me privately to tell him how far he had succeeded in his experiments. Not wishing to say anything disagreeable, I evaded the question to the best of my ability, answering with some vague generalities, but indicating sufficiently that it was not agreeable to be more explicit. He pressed me, however, to tell him candidly and explicitly whether he had succeeded, and how far. I then told him frankly that he had failed point-blank in every case. "Ah," said he, "you are skeptical." "No, sir," said I, "skepticism implies doubt, and I have no longer any doubts on the subject. *My skepticism is entirely removed!*"

XXIV.

NORMAL SCHOOLS.

THE term Normal School is an unfortunate misnomer, and its general adoption has led to much confusion of ideas. The word "Normal," from the Latin *norma*, a rule or pattern to work by, does not differ essentially from "Model." A Normal School, according to the meaning of the word, would be a pattern school, an institution which could be held up for imitation, to be copied by other schools of the same grade. But this meaning of the word is not what we mean by the thing. When we mean a school to be copied or imitated, we call it a Model School. Here the name and the thing agree. The name explains the thing. It is very different when we speak of a Normal School. To the uninitiated, the term either conveys no meaning at all; or, if your hearer is a man of letters, it conveys to him an idea which you have at once to explain away. You have to tell him, in effect, that a Normal School is not a Normal School, and then that it is something else, which the word does not in the least describe.

What then do we mean by a Normal School? What is the thing which we have called by this unfortunate name?

A Normal School is a seminary for the professional

education of teachers. It is an institution in which those who wish to become teachers learn how to do their work; in which they learn, not reading, but how to teach reading; not penmanship, but how to teach penmanship; not grammar, but how to teach grammar; not geography, but how to teach geography; not arithmetic, but how to teach arithmetic. The idea which lies at the basis of such an institute, is that knowing a thing, and knowing how to teach that thing to others, are distinguishable and very different facts. The knowledge of the subjects to be taught, may be gained at any school. In order to give to the Teachers' Seminary its full power and efficiency, it were greatly to be desired that the subjects themselves, as mere matters of knowledge, should be first learned elsewhere, before entering the Teachers' School. This latter would then have to do only with its own special function, that of showing its matriculants how to use these materials in the process of teaching. Unfortunately, we have not yet made such progress in popular education as to be able to separate these two functions to the extent that is desirable. Many of those who attend a Teachers' Seminary, come to it lamentably ignorant of the common branches of knowledge. They have consequently first to study these branches in the Normal School, as they would study them in any other school. That is, they have first to learn the facts as matters of knowledge, and then to study the art and science of teaching these facts to others. Instead of coming with their brick and mortar ready prepared, that they may be instructed in the use of the trowel and the plumb-line, they have to make their brick and mix their mortar after they enter the institution. This is undoubtedly a drawback and a misfortune. But it cannot be helped at present. All we can do is to define clearly the true idea of the Teachers' School, and then to work towards it as fast and as far as we can.

A Normal School is essentially unlike any other school. It has been compared indeed to those professional schools which are for the study of law, divinity, medicine, mining, engineering, and so forth. The Normal School, it is true, is like these schools in one respect. It is established with reference to the wants of a particular profession. It is a professional school. But those schools have for their main object the communication of some particular branch of science. They teach law, divinity, medicine, mining, or engineering. They aim to make lawyers, divines, physicians, miners, engineers, not teachers of these branches. The Professor in the. Law School aims, not to make Professors of law, but lawyers. The medical Professor aims, not to make medical lecturers, but practitioners. To render these institutions analogous to the Teachers' Seminary, their pupils should first study law, medicine, engineering, and so forth, and then sit at the feet of their Gamaliels to be initiated into the secrets of the Professorial chair, that they may in turn become Professors of those branches to classes of their own. Nor would such a plan, if it were possible, be altogether without its value. It surely needs no demonstration to prove, that in the highest departments, no less than in the lowest, something more than knowledge is needed in order to teach. An understanding of how to communicate one's knowledge, and practical skill in doing it, are as necessary in teaching theology, metaphysics, languages, infinitesimal analysis, or chemistry, as they are in teaching the alphabet. If there are bunglers, who know not how to go to work to teach a child its letters, or to open its young mind and heart to the reception of truth, whose school-rooms are places where the young mind and heart are in a state, either of perpetual torpor, or of perpetual nightmare, have these bunglers no analogues in the men of ponderous erudition that sometimes fill the Professor's chair? Have we no examples, in our highest seminaries of learning, of men very eminent in scientific attainments, who have not in themselves the first elements of a teacher? who impart to their students no quickening impulse? whose vast and towering knowledge may make them perhaps a grand feature in their College, attracting to it all eyes, but whose intellectual treasures, for all the practical wants of the students, are of no more use, than are the swathed and buried mummies in the pyramid of Cheops!

A Teachers' Seminary, if it were complete, would include in its curriculum of study the entire cycle of human knowledge, so far as it is taught by schools. Our teachers of mathematics and of logic, of law and of medicine, need indeed a knowledge of the branches which they are to teach, and for this knowledge they do not need a Teachers' Seminary. But they need something more than this knowledge. Besides being men of erudition, they need to be teachers, no less than the humbler members of the profession, who have only to teach the alphabet and the multiplication table; and there is in all teaching, high or low, something that is common to them all—an art and a skill which is different from the mere knowledge of the subjects; which is not necessarily learned in learning the subjects; which requires special, superadded gifts, and distinct study and training. There is, according to my observation, as great a lack of this special skill in the higher seminaries of learning, as in the lower seminaries. Were it possible to have a Normal School, not which should undertake to teach the entire encyclopædia of the sciences, but which, limiting itself to its one main function of developing the art and mystery of communicating knowledge, should turn out College Professors, and even Divinity, Law, and Medical Professors,—men who were really skilful teachers,—it would work a change in those venerable institutions as marked and decisive as that which it is now effecting in the common schools. Of course, no such scheme is possible; certainly, none such is contemplated. But I am very sure I shall not be considered calumnious, when I express the conviction, that there are learned and eminent occupants of Professors' chairs, who might find great benefit in an occasional visit to a good Normal School, or even to the class-room of a teacher trained in a Normal School. I certainly have seen, in the very lowest department of the common school, a style of teaching, which, for a wise and intelligent comprehension of its object, and for its quickening power upon the intellect and conscience, would compare favorably with the very best teaching I have ever seen in a College or University.

I come back, then, to the point from which I set out,

namely, that a Normal School, or Teachers' Seminary, differs essentially from every other kind of school. It aims to give the knowledge and skill that are needed alike in all schools. To make the point a little plainer, let me restate, with what clearness I can, some of the elementary truths and facts which lie at the foundation of the whole subject. Though to many of my readers it may be going over a beaten track, it may not be so to all; and we all do well, even in regard to known and admitted truths, to bring them occasionally afresh to the mind.

As it has been already said, a man may know a thing perfectly, and yet not be able to teach it. Of course, a man cannot teach what he does not know. He must first have the knowledge. But the mere possession of knowledge does not make one a teacher, any more than the possession of powder and shot makes him a marksman, or the possession of a rod and line makes him an angler. The most learned men are often unfortunately the very men who have least capacity for communicating what they know. Nor is this incapacity confined to those versed in book knowledge. It is common to every class of men, and to every kind of knowledge. Let me give an example. The fact about to be stated, was communicated to me by a gentleman of eminent commercial standing in Philadelphia, at that time the President of one of its leading banks. The fact occurred in his own personal experience. He was, at the time of its occurrence, largely engaged in the cloth trade. His faculties of mind and body, and particularly his sense of touch, had been so trained in this business, that in going rapidly over an invoice of cloth, as his eye and hand passed in quick succession from piece to piece, in the most miscellaneous assortment, he could tell instantly the value of each, with a degree of precision, and a certainty of knowledge, hardly credible. A single glance of the eye, a single touch, transient as thought, gave the result. His own knowledge of the subject, in short, was perfect, and it was rapidly winning him a fortune. Yet when undertaking to explain to a younger and less experienced member of the craft, whom he wished to befriend, by what process he arrived at his judgment, in other words, to teach what he knew, he found himself utterly at a loss. His thoughts had never run in that direction. "Oh!" said he, "you have only——to look at the cloth, and—and—to run your fingers over it,—thus. You will perceive at once the difference between one piece and another." It seems never to have occurred to him that another man's sensations and perceptions might in the same circumstances be quite different from his, and that in order to communicate his knowledge to one uninitiated, he must pause to analyze it; he must separate, classify, and name those several qualities of the cloth of which his senses took cognizance; he must then ascertain how far his interrogator perceived by his senses the same qualities which he himself did, and thus gradually get on common ground with him.

Let the receiving-teller of a bank be called upon to explain how it is that he knows at a glance a counterfeit bill from a genuine one, and in nine cases out of ten he will succeed no better than the cloth merchant did. Knowing and communicating what we know, doing and explaining what we do, are distinct, separable, and usually very different processes.

Similar illustrations might be drawn from artists, and from men of original genius in almost every profession, who can seldom give any intelligible account of how they achieve their results. The mental habits best suited for achievement are rarely those best suited for teaching. Marlborough, so celebrated for his military combinations, could never give any intelligible account of his plans. He had arrived at his conclusions with unerring certainty, but he was so little accustomed to observing his own mental processes, that he utterly failed in attempting to make them plain to others. He saw the points himself with perfect clearness, but he had no power to make others see them. To all objections to his plans, he could only say, "Silly, silly, that 's silly." It was much the same with Cromwell. It is so with most men who are distinguished for action and achievement. Patrick Henry would doubtless have made but a third-rate teacher of elocution, and old Homer but an indifferent lecturer on the art of poetry.

To acquire knowledge ourselves, then, and to put others in possession of what we have acquired, are not only distinct intellectual processes, but they are quite unlike. In the former case, the faculties merely go out towards the objects to be known, as in the case of the cloth merchant passing his eye and finger over the bales of cloth. But in the case of one attempting to teach, several additional processes are needed, besides that of collecting knowledge. He must turn his thoughts inward, so as to arrange and classify properly the contents of his intellectual storehouse. He must then examine his own mind, his intellectual machinery, so as to understand exactly how the knowledge came in upon himself. He must lastly study the minds of his pupils, so as to know through what channels the knowledge may best reach them. The teacher may not always be aware that he does all these things, that is, he may not always have a theory of his own art. But the art itself he must have. He must first get the knowledge of the things to be taught; he must secondly study his knowledge; he must thirdly study himself; he must lastly study his pupil. He is a teacher at all only so far as he does at least these four things.

In a Normal School, as before said, the knowledge of the subject is presupposed. The object of the Normal School is, not so much to make arithmeticians and grammarians, for instance, as to make teachers of arithmetic and grammar. This teaching faculty is a thing by itself, and quite apart from the subject matter to be taught. It underlies every branch of knowledge, and every trade and profession. The theologian, the mathematician, the linguist, the learned professor, no less than the teacher of the primary school, or of the Sabbath-school, all need this supplementary knowledge and skill, in which consists the very essence of teaching. This knowledge of how to teach is not acquired by merely studying the subject to be taught. It is a study by itself. A man may read familiarly the *Mechanique Celeste*, and yet not know how to teach the multiplication table. He may read Arabic or Sanskrit, and not know how to teach a child the alphabet of his mother tongue. The Sabbath-school teacher may dip deep into biblical lore, he may ransack the commentaries, and may become, as many Sabbath-school teachers are, truly learned in Bible knowledge, and yet be utterly incompetent to teach a class of children. He can no more hit the wandering attention, or make a lodgment of his knowledge in the minds of his youthful auditory, than the mere unskilled possessor of a fowling-piece can hit a bird upon the wing.

The art of teaching is the one indispensable qualification of the teacher. Without this, whatever else he may be, he is no teacher. How may this art be acquired? In the first place, many persons pick it up, just as they pick up a great many other arts and trades,—in a hap-hazard sort of way. They have some natural aptitude for it, and they grope their way along, by guess and by instinct, and through many failures, until they become good teachers, they hardly know how. To rescue the art from this condition of uncertainty and chance, is the object of the Normal School. In such a school, the main object of the pupil is to learn how to make others know what he himself knows. The whole current of his thoughts and studies is turned into this channel. Studying how to teach, with an experimental class to practise on, forms the constant topic of his meditations. It is surprising how rapidly, under such conditions, the faculty of teaching is developed; how fertile the mind becomes in devising practical expedients, when once the attention is roused and fixed upon the precise object to be attained, and the idea of what teaching really is, fairly has possession of the mind. For this purpose every well-ordered Normal School has, in connection with it, as a part of its organization, a Model School, to serve the double purpose of a school of observation and practice.

Thus, after these pupil-teachers are once familiar with the branches to be taught, and after they have become acquainted with the theory of teaching, as a science, it is surprising how soon, with even a little of this practice-teaching, they acquire the art. If the faculty of teaching is in them at all, a very few experimental lessons, under the eye of an experienced teacher, will develop it.

The fact of possessing within one's self this gift, or power of teaching, sometimes breaks upon the possessor himself with all the force of a surprising and most delightful discovery. The good teacher does not indeed stop here. He goes on to improve in his art, as long as he lives. But his greatest single achievement is when he takes the first step, —when he first learns to teach at all. The pupil of a Normal School gains there a start and an impulse, which carry him forward the rest of his life. A very little judicious experimental training redeems hundreds of candidates from utter and hopeless incompetency, and converts for them an awkward and painful drudgery into keen, hopeful and productive labor.

XXV.

PRACTICE-TEACHING.

ONE feature of a Normal School which distinguishes it especially from other schools, is the opportunity given to its matriculants for practising their art under the guidance and criticism of an experienced teacher. This practice-teaching is done in a Model School, maintained for this purpose in connection with the main school. Such is the theory.

But serious difficulties are encountered in carrying the plan into practical effect, and these difficulties are so great as in some instances to have led to the entire abandonment of the plan, while very rarely have the conductors of Normal schools been able to realize results in this matter commensurate with their wishes or with their views of what was desirable and right.

Some of the difficulties are the following: Parents who send their children to the Model School object to have their children taught to any considerable extent by mere pupil-teachers. The teachers of the Model School, having little or no acquaintance with the Normal pupils sent to teach under their supervision, do not feel that entire freedom in criticising the performance which is essential to its success. The irregularities produced by these practice-teachings have a tendency to impair the discipline of the classes in the Model School.

For these and other reasons which I need not dwell upon, I at least have always been obliged to be somewhat chary in regard to the amount of practice-teaching that was done in the institution under my care, and have never felt quite satisfied as to the result. At the beginning of the year 1867, I determined to try the plan of having a considerable portion of the practice-teaching done in the Normal School itself, the Model School still holding its place in the system as furnishing an unrivalled opportunity for observation, and to some extent of practice also. The effect of thus extending the opportunity for practice by including the Normal School in its operations has been most happy. The pupils have attained a degree of freedom in the exercise which is working the most marked and decisive results. They enter into it with more zest than into any other exercise of the class, and derive from it in some instances as much benefit as from all their other exercises put together.

Some detailed account of the method may perhaps be of interest to other laborers in the same field. The method is substantially the same as that followed in the Girls High and Normal School of Philadelphia, from which indeed I borrowed the idea.

Once a week I make up a programme containing the names of those who are to teach during the following week, and the classes and lessons which they are severally to teach. The practice-pupils are thus enabled to prepare themselves fully for the exercise. It is an indispensable condition in all these exercises that the lesson be given without the use of the book. When a pupil enters a room to teach one of these assigned lessons, he is to bring with him only his crayon and pointer, and is expected to assume entire charge of the class, maintaining order, hearing the pupils recite, correcting their mistakes, illustrating the subject, if necessary, by diagrams or experiments, giving supplementary information drawn from other sources than the text-book, and acting in all respects as if he were the regular teacher. The regular teacher meanwhile sits by, observing in silence, and at the close of the day writes out a full and detailed criticism upon the performance in a book kept for this purpose, and gives the pupil an average for it, the maximum being 100. These criticisms, together with the teaching averages, are read next day by the Principal to the pupil in the presence of the class to which he belongs, with additional comments in regard to any principles of teaching that may be involved in the criticisms.

An essential element of success in this scheme, is that the teachers should be thoroughly faithful in the work of criticism, and point out the errors and shortcomings of the young practitioners, not with harshness, but with unsparing truthfulness and wise discrimination. Practice-teaching under such conditions cannot fail to have a powerful effect. The pupils are stimulated by it to put forth the very best efforts of which they are capable, and the talent which they often develop is a surprise equally to themselves and their teachers.

I cannot better give an idea of this practice-teaching,

and especially of the criticism which is its vitalizing principle, than by quoting a few of the actual criticisms made during the last year. I feel sure they will interest teachers and perhaps the public.

In making these extracts, I suppress, of course, the names of the parties.

NOTES ON PRACTICE-TEACHING.

Miss —— gave the C class a lesson in Elocution. She was animated and energetic in giving the vocal exercises, but she pitched her voice too high. The same shrill tone characterized the concert reading. Many of the criticisms given by pupils were not loud enough to be heard by the whole class. One of the ladies, in giving a sketch of Shakspeare, said "his principal works *was* 'Much Ado About Nothing,' 'Merchant of Venice,' etc.;" but the error passed unnoticed by pupils and teacher. Miss —— herself, said "Hamlet thought it was n't *him*." She marked the pupils too high, the worst readers in the class receiving 8 and 9. Teaching average 85.

Miss —— gave the D class a lesson in History. She was herself well prepared with the lesson, but she allowed the pupils too long a time to think and *guess*. A chronology lesson is apt to be dry and uninteresting; and unless the teacher calls upon the pupils in *rapid* succession, thus keeping them wide awake, the interest will flag, and even good pupils will be inattentive. One of the pupils, after gaping two or three times, indulged in short naps during the recitation; the teacher evidently did not see her. Miss —— marked the pupils judiciously. Teaching average 90.

Miss —— gave the D class a lesson in Arithmetic. She assisted the pupils too much. She did not require them to be accurate enough in answering questions; otherwise she taught well, the subject being rather a difficult one. Miss —— marked the pupils judiciously. Teaching average 85.

Miss —— gave the D class a lesson in Grammar. She began the recitation well, spoke in a loud and decided tone, and was well prepared with the lesson. She failed to keep her class in order; she allowed pupils to speak without being called upon, and all to criticise and ask questions at the same instant—thus she became confused and sought refuge behind her book. Teaching average 80.

Miss —— gave the C class a lesson in the Constitution of the United States. She was too quiet in conducting the recitation. The entire period was spent in repeating the mere words of the book; but once or twice the lady asked for the explanation of clauses, and then the answers given were neither full nor satisfactory, yet the lady ventured no comment of her own. Many practical questions might have been given by the teacher respecting the executive departments, ambassadors, consuls, treaties, and so forth. The lesson contained many subjects of interest sufficient to occupy more than the allotted time. Teachers should call more frequently for definitions, and always take it for granted that their pupils are ignorant of the meaning of even the simplest words. I venture to assert that more than one third of the class left the room without knowing the difference between a *reprieve* and a *pardon*. Teaching average 80.

Miss —— gave the D class a lesson in Arithmetic. She was well prepared with the lesson, seemed to understand the subject fully, and readily answered questions proposed by pupils; but she allowed too many pupils to speak at once, and did not pay enough attention to *signs*. One of the pupils began a sentence with a small letter, and Miss —— took no notice of it. Miss —— marked judiciously. Teaching average 88.

Miss —— gave the C class a lesson in the Constitution. She failed entirely in teaching. She became embarrassed, and soon lost the respect and confidence of the class. Pupils assumed all sorts of positions; and one picked up a ruler and began fanning himself, but was not rebuked by the teacher. The lady, not familiar with the names of the scholars, made several mistakes, (perfectly excusable); but, there being no sympathy between the teacher and the class, the pupils laughed immoderately, and seemed to enjoy the lady's embarrassment. The words of the book were repeated over and over again, without a word of explanation or comment, until the teacher, tired of the monotony, announced that the lesson was finished, and called upon me to fill up the remainder of the time. The lesson was one that needed thorough preparation on the part of the teacher, but Miss —— had merely studied the *words* and not the *subject;* when asked a very simple question by one of the pupils, she was completely nonplussed. Teaching average 50.

Miss —— gave the D class a lesson in Map Drawing. She became somewhat confused in her work, and so did not distinctly enough give the points of criticism. I think she was not familiar enough with the map drawn to notice, with sufficient readiness, the great points of error in the work. Several of the pupils were allowed, in one or two cases, to speak at the same time. She marked well, using a good scale of markings. Teaching average 85.

Miss —— gave the D class a lesson in Arithmetic. She was either very careless or had not prepared the proper lesson, as she gave pupils problems to solve that were not in the lesson; in consequence of which some good pupils failed, as they had not prepared an advance lesson. She was too quiet, and spoke in so low a tone that many of the pupils did not hear her. The pupils were more animated than the teacher. Miss —— marked some pupils too high, others too low, and in one instance did not mark at all. Teaching average 65.

Miss —— gave the D class a lesson in History. She was thoroughly prepared with the lesson, and did not confine herself to the mere words of the text-book. She asked many good general questions connected with the subject, thus compelling pupils to think; and whenever the class failed to give the desired information, the lady very promptly gave it herself; she thus won the confidence of her pupils. Miss —— lacked animation and did not speak loud enough; otherwise she did well. Teaching average 92.

Miss —— gave the D class a lesson in Grammar. She has improved since teaching for me before, but she still lacks energy and decision. She gave the pupil who was reciting all her attention, thus allowing an opportunity to some (who took advantage of it) to assume lounging positions, in which to await lazily for their turn to recite. Some remained wide awake, and embarrassed Miss ——, by speaking at any time, even interrupting her in the middle of a sentence, to ask questions. Teaching average 87.

Miss —— gave the C class a lesson in Grammar. She taught well. She spoke in that decided tone which conveys a conviction of truth to pupils, and by so doing gained their confidence. She used the blackboards to advantage, and thoroughly inspected and criticised all writings that she had required to be put upon the boards. The facts she taught were correct, except one, which was, that "is ashamed" was a verb in the passive voice; in this she was corrected by a number of the class. Teaching average 93.

Miss —— gave the C class a lesson in Elocution. She failed in teaching. The pupils read badly, and many errors were made, but there were no criticisms. The lady spoke in a very low tone, and seemed to be afraid of the class. She did not read a single line for the pupils. Reading cannot be taught properly by arbitrary rules, the voice of the living teacher is indispensable. Teaching average 65.

Miss —— gave the D class a lesson in Elocution. She cannot become a successful teacher until she studies the pronunciation of words. Not only did she permit mistakes made by the pupils to pass unnoticed, but she mispronounced many words herself, hos-*pit*-a-ble, for *hos*-pi-ta-ble, *in*-tense for in-*tense*, etc.; the errors consisted chiefly in changing the accented syllable. In the word *machination*, however, though the accent was correctly marked, she taught the class to call it "mash-in-a-tion." There can be no possible excuse for such carelessness, or rather ignorance, since the lady had three days for the preparation of the lesson. The dictionary should be kept in constant use by pupils and teacher. Teaching average 65.

Miss —— gave the C class a lesson in the Constitution. She did well. The lesson was a long one, and somewhat difficult, but the lady evinced thorough preparation. She ought to have disturbed the repose of the drones in the class, by calling upon them more frequently. Explanations given by the teacher should be repeated by the pupils: first, to ascertain whether or not they have been properly understood, and secondly, to make a deeper impression upon the minds of the scholars. Indeed, the whole business of teaching might be summed up in two words, namely, *simplify* and *repeat.* Teaching average 95.

Miss —— gave the D class a lesson in Map Drawing. She was quite well prepared for the lesson, but did not always speak quite distinctly enough; she required all those pupils, who had criticisms to make, to stand, and then designated one to give them—a very good plan. Miss —— must be more careful in regard to the grammatical construction of her own sentences. Teaching average 90.

Miss —— gave the C class a lesson in Mental Arithmetic. She became somewhat confused, and so made several mistakes in her work. She attempted to solve several examples, but each time made some error, either of statement or solution. She was not careful enough in her markings, omitting to mark one of the pupils for absence, and two for recitation. Teaching average 88.

Miss —— gave the D class a lesson in Map-Drawing. She should have kept one of the divisions at the board drawing while the other were reciting. It was the first day of map description, she should therefore have given them an example of the work desired; instead of this she scolded them for not knowing her method. Teachers should be careful never to ask for anything but what the pupil would reasonably be expected to know. If you insist that they shall give anything not found in the lesson, or not before given by the teacher, they will become angry and careless, as shown in the class to-day. She did not criticise the map drawn. Teaching average, 82.

Miss —— gave the C class a lesson in Constitution. She did well. She used the blackboards to advantage, and very carefully examined and criticised the work placed there by the pupils. She should speak in a louder and more decided tone. Teaching average 93.

Miss —— gave the C class a lesson in Elocution. She gave a very short vocal exercise and omitted the concert reading. During the recitation she read *remarkably* well; her voice was clear and full, her emphasis and inflections were correct, and her whole manner free from embarrassment. The entrance of three or four visitors did not in the least disconcert her; for her calmness and dignity, she deserves much commendation. Teaching average 95.

Miss —— gave the D class a lesson in Geography. She taught well. She did not call upon enough members of the class for recitation. A subject that can be divided into portions small enough to enable the teacher to call upon each member of the class at each recitation, should be so divided. She made it still worse by calling upon several members to recite twice. With a little more energy on her part she could have had more work performed in the forty minutes. Teaching average 90.

Miss —— gave the D class a lesson in Arithmetic. She taught very well. The subject, Repetends, was a difficult one, which required careful preparation on the part of the teacher and close attention during the recitation. Miss ——, conscious of this, made herself perfectly familiar with the lesson before appearing in class, and when pupils failed to explain examples from a want of knowledge, she was ready and able to give the necessary information. She marked judiciously. Teaching average 90.

Miss —— gave the C class a lesson in Ancient History. She was sprightly and animated. She spoke in a clear, decided tone; but she pursued no regular plan in conducting the recitation. Events in Egyptian and Assyrian history were indiscriminately mixed, the pupils became confused, and the lady herself was somewhat bewildered. Teaching average 88.

Miss —— gave the D class a lesson in Grammar. She did not speak loud enough for the class to understand her. There was much disorder in the class, but no notice was taken of it by the teacher. Some carried on a conversation among themselves, others asked questions without permission, often at the most inappropriate times. Many errors passed unnoticed, and the lady gave corrections herself which she should have required of the pupils. Several times, in attempting to correct, she made the errors worse; for instance she parsed verbs that were transitive and in the passive voice as being intransitive and active. She must endeavor to gain more confidence in herself. Teaching average 75.

Miss —— gave the A class a lesson in Geometry. She taught the class decidedly well. She deserves all the more credit, as it was a difficult lesson of her own class. She allowed but one error of work—that I noticed—to pass uncorrected. Her method of calling upon the class for criticisms was very good. She should strive to speak a little more distinctly. Teaching average, 96.

Miss —— gave the B class a lesson in Physiology. She evinced perfect familiarity with the subject of the lesson. She did not confine herself to the text-book, but asked many good, general questions. One of the pupils did not understand a portion of the lesson which was to be explained by a diagram. Miss —— endeavored to make the matter clear by an explanation, which was very good, still the pupil did not see it clearly. I think the teacher would have succeeded in clearing the difficulty if she had used the *pointer* instead of designating certain points by letters. She spoke a little too low. Teaching average, 96.

Miss —— gave the D class a lesson in Geography. She deserves great credit for the distinctness with which she speaks, for her care in the preparation of the lesson for the day, and for the promptness with which she stops all irregularities in the class. Her marks for the day were a little too high; she did not make distinction enough between the good and the poor scholars. Teaching average, 96.

Miss —— gave the A class a lesson in Elocution. She succeeded admirably. The vocal exercises and concert reading were well given. The lady threw herself entirely into the work, and this was the real secret of her success. Her grade of marking was too high; otherwise, she did very well. Teaching average, 97.

Miss —— gave the A class a lesson in English Literature. She did not spend enough time upon the lesson for the day, and consumed too much of the period in reviewing old lessons. She was not careful in examining the blackboards. *Lbs.* was permitted to stand as the abbreviation for pounds sterling, and *whimsicalities* was spelled with two l's. The lady made no deduction for errors; all the pupils with but one exception received 10. She deserves commendation for speaking in a loud, clear tone. Teaching average, 88.

Miss —— gave the C class a lesson in Constitution. She did nothing more than hear the recitations. She did not venture to give any explanations or to ask them of the class, but spent the whole period in repeating again and again the words of the text-book. It is probable that no pupil knew anything more of the subject on going from the room than when she entered. Teachers should possess and impart to their pupils some information independent of the book. Teaching average, 55.

Miss —— taught the A class Geometry. She did not question enough or criticise enough, but almost always called upon the class for criticisms. She added no remarks or criticisms herself; thus many important omissions and errors were unnoticed. She succeeded well in calling upon almost every member of the class. Teaching average, 75.

Miss —— gave the B class a lesson in Physiology. She was not sufficiently animated and self-possessed. The substance of the lesson was recited before the expiration of the period, which left the lady at a loss to know what she should do with the remainder of the time. It might have been profitably employed asking questions of importance connected with the lesson; but instead of doing so, Miss —— turned to me for assistance. She was asked her opinion of a disputed point, which, although of slight importance, merited some attention; but she passed it by, notwithstanding her attention was called to it several times. Teaching average, 76.

Miss —— gave the A class a lesson in Elocution. She displayed the tact and skill of an experienced teacher. She assumed full authority over the pupils (though they were her classmates), and her whole manner was such that a visitor entering the room would have supposed she was the permanent teacher. One secret of her success was that she had given the reading lesson much home practice and preparation. Teaching average, 100.

Miss —— taught the A class in Literature. She taught well. Though rather quiet, she succeeded in awakening the interest of her pupils, and the entire recitation was very animated. The class is a good one, and the pupils deserve as much commendation as the teacher. Teaching average, 96.

Miss —— gave the D class a lesson in Geography. She came before the class well prepared for her duties. She did not use the book, though it was written in the catechetical style — the one most difficult to teach without some such reference. She by her questions brought out a number of points not given in the text-book. Teaching average, 97.

Miss —— gave the B class a lesson in Rhetoric. She showed a thorough preparation of the lesson and taught well. She should have worked a little faster. Pupils were allowed too much time to think. Teaching average, 98.

Miss —— gave the D class a lesson in History. She taught with much dignity and self-possession. She did not teach simply by having the lesson recited as the author had given it, but asked for the definition of words, and gave information not found in the text-book. But one error was allowed to pass, which was that of calling Queen Victoria the grand-daughter of William of Orange. Teaching average, 98.

Miss —— gave the B class a lesson in Physiology. She conducted the recitation in a very dignified and lady-like manner. The lesson was a difficult one, but the teacher seemed to understand the subject thoroughly. There was a reference to the *retina* of the eye in the lesson; the pupils not having studied that subject, did not know what the retina was, and called upon the teacher for explanation; she attempted to describe it, but failed to make them understand because she did not thoroughly understand it herself. With this exception, she taught very well. Teaching average, 96.

Miss —— gave the B class a lesson in Elocution. She is a good teacher, and reads well. She maintained her dignity and composure during the entire recitation, though several visitors were present. Nothing tends to embarrass a teacher so much as the entrance of strangers; the lady's calmness and self-possession then are worthy of much commendation. Teaching average 100.

Miss —— gave the C class a lesson in Mental Arithmetic. She read the questions distinctly, and had them correctly solved; but for the plan of recitation, she helped the pupils too much. The method was that called "Chance Assignment;" in this method, as the pupils have time to think of the problems, the work should be purely that of the memory, in regard to the example itself. Teaching average 95.

Miss —— gave the A class a lesson in Literature. She evinced thorough preparation, and displayed considerable tact in conducting the recitation. Every pupil was called on and compelled to recite or confess ignorance. Teaching average 98.

Miss —— gave the C class a lesson in Elocution. She selected a very difficult reading-lesson, and not only read it well herself, but insisted upon the pupils reading it well too. The lady has a good clear voice, but it lacks power; nothing will develop this quality but constant daily practice. Teaching average 97.

Miss —— taught the C class in Ancient History. She did not succeed. Her embarrassment was caused in a great measure by not knowing the names of the pupils. Teachers should obtain lists of the names, if they are not familiar with them. The lesson being one in mythology, could have been made very interesting with a slight effort on the part of the teacher. Many errors in pronunciation made by both teacher and pupils, were allowed to pass, Teaching average 72.

Miss —— gave the A class a lesson in Elocution. She taught well, but would have succeeded better if she had given the lesson a little more home practice. When delivering a passage requiring considerable force, she heightened the pitch of her voice, and thus gave an unpleasant shrillness, where the pure orotund tone was needed. Teaching average 95.

Miss —— gave the B class a lesson in Elocution. She is a very sprightly, animated teacher, and reads well. She paid special attention to the correct orthoëpy of words, and insisted upon pupils' making use of their dictionaries whenever a word occurred with which they were not familiar. Teaching average 100.

Miss —— gave the D class a lesson in History. She is one of the best teachers in her class. She is sprightly, animated, and critical. The lesson was well taught; a map having been neatly drawn on the board, the teacher required the most important places referred to in the lesson, to be pointed out upon it. Teaching average 100.

Miss —— gave the A class a lesson in Chemistry. She has improved very much in teaching. She understood the subject which she taught, and had given the lesson careful preparation. She requested one of the pupils to look for the orthoëpy of a word which occurred in the lesson. The lady turned over the leaves of the dictionary in a very careless manner, then took her seat, saying she could not find the word, although she must have been conscious all the while that she was not searching for it in the proper place. Miss ——, instead of sending the lady to look for the word again, as she should have done, pronounced it herself. The teacher should require prompt obedience on the part of pupils. Teaching average 95.

Miss —— gave the C class a lesson in Elocution. She is a very energetic teacher, and manifests a deep interest in her pupils—hence, her success. A visitor would have inferred from her manner, that she was the permanent teacher, not a mere substitute for a passing hour. Teaching average, 100.

XXVI.

ATTENTION AS A MENTAL FACULTY, AND AS A MEANS OF MENTAL CULTURE.

THE illustrations which first led to a satisfactory elucidation of the subject, were drawn from the eye. There are many facts in the history of vision, which show that we may experience sensations and perceptions and other intellectual operations, and may at the time be conscious of the same, without giving them any attention, or, at least, without giving them such a degree of attention as to have the slightest recollection of them afterwards.

When, for instance, we read a printed book, the eye glances so rapidly from sentence to sentence, that we can hardly persuade ourselves that we actually see successively every letter. We certainly have no recollection of having gone through such an innumerable train of conscious acts as the theory necessarily implies. That such, however, is the case, is proved by the fact, that if by accident any letter is omitted, or transposed, or put upside down, the eye at once detects the mistake. The fact is familiar to all. It can be accounted for only on the supposition that, even in the rapid and cursory perusal of a book, the eye actually passes from letter to letter, and gives to each a distinct notice. It not only notices each letter, but the position of each in reference to the other letters in the line, and even those nice diacritical points by which one letter is distinguished from another, as *c* from *e*, *u* from *n*, *b* from *d*, *p* from *q*. This notice, however, is so slight, the transition is so rapid, that we have no recollection of it afterwards, and we can hardly persuade ourselves that such has been the sober and yet most wonderful fact.

Take another instance. If, on the occasion of an evening assemblage, by a sudden movement of the gas-pipe, any one should instantly extinguish all the lights in the room and leave the building for a time in total darkness, and if, by an equally sudden movement, he should then restore the light to its previous condition, every one present would notice the change and have a distinct recollection of it afterwards. Yet, every time we close our eyes in winking, that is, several times in every minute of our waking hours, we experience precisely this change from full and perfect vision to total darkness. But no one ever notices or remembers the fact of his winking, unless he stops to make it the subject of special attention.

Sight however is not the only means of illustrating this point. We are drawn to a similar conclusion by observing the workings of the mind itself, in the act of volition. Whenever we make any single volition an object of special attention, we are conscious of that volition, and we have a distinct recollection of it afterwards. Yet probably not one out of ten thousand, possibly not one out of a million, of our simple volitions, is ever known to us after the moment of its occurrence. In voluntary muscular action, every distinct movement requires a distinct volition. And how innumerable are the movements necessary to the accomplishment of any one of the ordinary purposes of life! We sit down for example to write a letter to a friend. The nimble pen dances from point to point over the darkening page, and when we reach the bottom, we have not the least recollection of having willed any one of those countless muscular movements which have been necessary to what, but for its every-day occurrence, would be accounted the greatest feat of legerdemain ever performed by man!

Take for example the act of reading aloud. Every letter requires for its utterance at least one distinct muscular contraction. Some letters require several. Now it has been found on trial that we are able to pronounce more than a thousand letters in a minute. That is, during every minute that we are reading aloud, we perform between one and two thousand distinct muscular movements, and by necessity a like number of antecedent acts of the will, to say nothing of those other acts, not less numerous in the case of a speaker, connected with the general movement of the body in earnest gesticulation. Yet after the hour's performance, what does the speaker or the reader remember of all these countless volitions? Nothing but the one general purpose to please, instruct, or persuade an audience.

The conclusion, toward which these illustrations point, is objected to by some writers, on the ground of the incredible rapidity which it attributes to our intellectual operations. Is it possible, it is asked, that we can crowd into such a space of time so many acts of the will, and that we are, at the moment when each happens, conscious of its presence? Is it not more probable that these rapid muscular actions are resolvable, in some way, into the law of habit? May they not become in some sense mechanical and automatic, so as to require no intervention of the will? Take for example, the case of a person learning to play upon a musical instrument. The first step is to move the fingers from key to key with a slow motion, looking at the notes, and exerting an express act of volition at every note. By degrees, however, the motions somehow cling to each other, and to the impressions of the notes, in the way of associations, the acts of volition all the while growing less and less express, until at last they become quite evanescent and imperceptible. An expert will play from notes or from memory, and with a rapidity of motion that is perfectly bewildering, while at the same time he himself is carrying on quite a different train of thoughts in his mind, or even perhaps holding a conversation with another. Hence, it is concluded, by the writers referred to, that in these cases there is really no intervention of that idea or state of the mind called will.

The authorities for this hypothesis are among the highest that can be named in the history of intellectual science. Let us see how far the hypothesis explains the facts of the case. The most rapid performer, it is obvious, can at any time retard his execution, until his movements become so slow that each one may be made, as originally it was made, the subject of special attention, and may be distinctly remembered afterwards. Now, according to the hypothesis proposed, we will our actions, and are conscious both of the act, and the antecedent volition, so long as their rapidity is confined to a certain rate; but, as soon as the rapidity exceeds that rate, the operation is taken out of our hands, and is carried on by some unknown power, of which we know no more than we do of the circulation of the blood, or of the systole and diastole of the heart! Such a supposition is about as reasonable as it would be to say that a projectile passes through the intermediate space, when it is thrown with such a moderate degree of velocity that we can see it, in its progress; but, when it is thrown with such velocity as to become invisible, it ceases to pass through the intermediate space, and reaches the goal only because projectiles have the habit of doing so!

The hypothesis then breaks down, and we are forced back to our original supposition, namely, that those actions which are voluntary originally, never cease to be so; that when, as in the cases supposed, we retain no recollection of particular volitions, it is because of some law of our nature by which we are capable of recollecting only those acts upon which the attention has been fixed with a certain degree of intensity and for some perceptible space of time; that the volition, in other words, is too feeble and too rapid to leave any impression on the memory. To argue that there has been no volition, because we do not recollect it, is as absurd as it would be to say that there has been no muscular act, because in many cases we have as little recollection of the muscular act, as we have of the antecedent volition.

Besides, there are many other mental acts, as rapid as those which have been adduced,—so rapid that not the least recollection of them remains,—where, yet, this mechanical or automatic hypothesis affords not the least explanation. Thus the expert accountant in a Bank adds up a long column of figures with the same rapidity and ease with which ordinary persons would read a passage from a familiar author, and he brings out in the end the exact sum, which he can do in no other way than by taking note in passing of the precise character and value of each figure. Yet, at the end of such a process, the accountant has no more recollection of those rapidly succeeding acts of the mind, than has the musical performer of those countless volitions put forth in the course of a piece of brilliant musical instrumentation.

As to the objection, that the theory attributes an almost inconceivable rapidity to some of our mental operations, it may be answered, in the first place, that there is no reason, surely, why mind should not be capable of as rapid action as its handmaid, matter; and, in the second place, that our ideas of time are relative, quite as much as our ideas of space; and if the microscope has revealed a world of wonders too minute in point of space to be observed by the naked eye, in whose existence we yet believe with undoubting confidence, we may without greater difficulty believe in the existence of mental acts crowded into so narrow a point of time, so rapid and transitory in their occurrence, as to leave no impression upon the memory.

The facts which have been adduced, then, teach clearly two things: first, that by far the greatest part of what we do and experience and are necessarily conscious of at the time of their occurrence, immediately fade from the recollection, as shadows pass over a landscape; and secondly, that in order to the recollection of any act or object, it is necessary that the mind be fixed upon it for some perceptible space of time and with some sensible degree of attention. It is this indissoluble connection of the attention with memory, this absolute dependence of the latter upon the former, which gives the subject such far-reaching import in considering the means of intellectual culture.

How it is that we are able to exclude all subjects but one from the thoughts, is not very easy of explanation. It is obvious that we cannot do it by direct volition. The very fact of our willing not to attend to a particular object, fixes our attention upon it. That we have, however, some power and agency in fixing our attention on one object and in withdrawing it from another, is a fact within the knowledge and experience of every one, whether we can explain the mode by which it is done or not. We have the power of what the chemists call "elective affinity;" we make our choice of some one of the various objects claiming the attention, and fix it upon that; and it seems to be a law of our nature, that when we thus direct the attention to one object, all others, of themselves, and by some natural necessity, retire from the thoughts. This is as near an approach, probably, as we shall ever make, towards an exact verbal expression of a fact, for an intimate knowledge of which, after all, every man must refer to his own consciousness.

This power of singling out and fastening upon some one object to the exclusion of all others,—in other words, this power of attention — exists in almost infinite degrees in different individuals. The degree in which it exists is the measure of a man's intellectual stature. No man can be truly great who does not possess it to a high degree. To command our attention is to command ourselves, to be truly master of our own powers and resources.

The subject, then, becomes one of first importance in every kind of either mental or moral improvement. Its vital connection with the faculty of memory has been already suggested. Perhaps, however, this branch of the subject should be set forth with a little more distinctness. There are many vague, dreamy notions afloat on the subject of memory, standing comparisons and metaphors, intended to illustrate its uses and magnify its importance, but not declaring with any degree of precision what it is. It is called, for instance, the "storehouse of our ideas." The metaphor conveys undoubtedly a certain amount of truth in regard to the subject. At the same time, there are some important particulars, in which the comparison, for it is nothing more, conveys a wrong impression. Experience teaches us, for instance, that recollections, unlike other articles of store, are from the time of their deposit undergoing a continual process of decay, and if they do not fade entirely from the mind, it is because we occasionally bring them anew under the review of the mind, and thus restore them to their original freshness and vigor.

Dismissing, therefore, the metaphor, I shall, I presume, express with sufficient accuracy the established doctrine on this subject by the following statements: that of the great multitude of mental operations which we experience, by far the larger part perish at the moment of their birth;

that others, to which for any reason we give, at the time of their occurrence, some sufficient degree of attention, afterwards recur to us, or are in some way present to our thoughts; that this recurrence of former ideas to our thoughts is sometimes spontaneous, without any voluntary action on our part, and sometimes the consequence of a direct effort of the will; and lastly, that the capacity which we have of being thus revisited by former thoughts is called memory, while the thoughts themselves, which thus return, are called memories, or more commonly recollections.

How it is that by an act of volition we can summon again into the mind an idea which has formerly been present, and which is now absent, we have the same difficulty in explaining which we had in explaining how, by an act of volition, we can banish a thought which is now present, or by the power of attention can detain some one thought to the exclusion of all others. To think what particular thing it is that we wish to remember, is in fact to have remembered it already. It is an obstruse and difficult inquiry, into which it is not necessary now to enter. A more important inquiry, and one connected directly with our present theme, relates to the different kinds of memory, and their connection severally with the faculty of attention.

Quickness of memory is that quality which is most easily developed, especially in young persons. It is also its most showy quality, and the temptation to give it an inordinate development is strong. The habit of getting things by rote, is easily acquired by practice. It is astonishing what masses of Scripture texts young children will get by heart, when under some special stimulus of reward or display. I have often refused to publish marvellous feats of this kind, not because I thought the accounts incredible, (unfortunately, they were too true,) but because I thought they were a species of mental excess, and they should no more be encouraged than bodily excesses. A little girl in my own Sunday-School once actually committed to memory the whole of the Westminster Assembly's Shorter Catechism in three days! Six months afterwards she hardly knew a word of it. It had been a regular mental debauch. A few more such atrocities would have made her an idiot. College records tell us of what are called "crammed men," that is, men who literally stuff themselves with knowledge in order to pass a particular examination, or to gain a particular honor, and who afterwards forget their knowledge, as fast as they have acquired it. There is a well authenticated instance of a student who actually learned the six books of Euclid by heart, though he could not tell the difference between an angle and a triangle. The memory of such men is quickened like that of the parrot. They learn purely by rote. Real mental attention, the true digester of knowledge, is never roused. The knowledge which they gorge, is never truly assimilated and made their own.

A quality of memory vastly more important than quickness, is tenacity. To hold on to what we get, is the secret of mental, no less than of pecuniary accumulations. The mind, too, like other misers, clings most tenaciously to that which has cost it most labor. Come lightly, go lightly, the world over. Knowledge which comes into the mind without toil and effort, without protracted and laborious attention, is apt to go as easily as it came.

But, by far the most important quality of memory, for the practical purposes of life, is readiness. Like quickness and tenacity, it is to be greatly improved, if not acquired by practice. It is in the cultivation of this quality, that the power of a good teacher shines forth most conspicuously. Quickness and tenacity may be cultivated by solitary study. But readiness requires for its development a live teacher, and the stir of the school-room and the class. Here it is that the art of questioning shows its wonderful resources. Repeated and continued interrogatories, judiciously worded, have a sort of talismanic power. They oblige the scholar to bring out his knowledge from its hidden recesses, to turn it over and over, and inside out, and upside down, to look at it and to handle it, so that not only it becomes forever and indestructibly his own, but he can ever afterwards use it at will with the same readiness that he uses his hands or his eyes. This is what a skilful teacher may do for his scholars, by a knowledge and practice of the art of questioning. Unfortunately, teachers in general find it much easier passively to hear a lesson, than to muster as much intellectual energy as is necessary to ask a question.

It was a remark of Bacon's, that, if we wish to commit anything to memory, we will accomplish more in ten readings, if at each perusal we make the attempt to repeat it from memory, referring to the book only when the memory fails, than we would by a hundred readings made in the ordinary way, and without any intervening trials.

The explanation of this fact is, that each effort to recollect the passage secures to the subsequent perusal a more intense degree of attention; and it seems to be a law of our nature, not only that there is no memory without attention, which I have labored at some length to establish, but that the degree of memory is in a great measure proportioned to the degree of the attention.

You will see at once the bearing of this fact upon that species of intellectual dissipation, called "general reading," in which the mental voluptuary reads merely for momentary excitement, in the gratification of an idle curiosity, and which is as enervating and debilitating to the intellectual faculties, as other kinds of dissipation are to the bodily functions. One book, well read and thoroughly digested, nay, one single train of thought, carefully elaborated and attentively considered, is worth more than any conceivable amount of that indolent, dreamy sort of reading in which many persons indulge. There is in fact no more unsafe criterion of knowledge than the number of books a man has read. A young man once told me he had read the entire list of publications of the American Sunday-School Union. He was about as wise as the man at the hotel, who began at the top of the bill of fare with the intention of eating straight through to the bottom! Depend upon it, this mental gorging is debilitating and debauching alike to the moral and the intellectual constitution. There is too much reading even of good books. No one should ever read a book, without subsequent meditation or conversation about it, and an attempt to make the thoughts his own, by a vigorous process of mental assimilation. Any continuous intellectual occupation, which does not leave us wiser and stronger, most assuredly will leave us weaker, just as filling the body with food which it does not digest, only makes it feeble and sickly. We are the worse for reading any book, if we are not the better for it.

There is an obvious distinction on this subject, of some practical importance, first suggested, so far as I am aware, by the Scotch metaphysician, Dr. Reid, between attention as directed to external objects, and the same faculty directed to what passes within us. When we attend to what is without us, to what we hear, or see, or smell, or taste, or touch, the process is called observation. When, on the other hand, dismissing for the time all notice of the external world, we turn our thoughts inward, and consider only what is passing in the inner chambers of the mind,—when, for instance, we analyze our motives, or notice the workings of passion, or scan the mysterious and subtle agency of the will, the process is called reflection. This latter species of attenion is one much more difficult of development than the former. It is developed ordinarily much later in life,—seldom, I believe, developed to any considerable extent before the age of manhood,—developed by some professions and pursuits much more than by others,—and in a very large class of mankind, probably the majority, never developed at all.

This species of attention, which is thus directed inwards, subjective attention some would call it,—in other words, the reflective powers,—are, I doubt not, capable of being cultivated much earlier in life than the age which I have

indicated as the normal period of their development. I am constrained, however, in opposition to many high authorities in education, to doubt the wisdom of a precocious cultivation of this part of our intellectual system. In all our plans of education, we should closely follow nature, who seems to have reserved the judgment and the reflective powers for the latest, as they certainly are the most perfect, of her endowments. We, who are teachers, have chiefly to do with those whose powers are as yet immature, and whose attention is to be cultivated primarily in its direction to external objects. Our business, in other words, is to train our pupils first of all to habits of observation.

In doing this, it is of some practical importance to bear in mind the well-known difference, in respect to memory, between the objects of different senses. Whether it be attributed to the different degrees of perfection with which the qualities of bodies are perceived, or to some difference in the qualities themselves, or whatever may be the cause, the fact is established beyond a question, that the knowledge which comes to us through the medium of the eye is of all kinds of knowledge the most easily and the most perfectly remembered. We remember, indeed, the temperature of one day as distinguished from that of another; we remember the sound of a voice; we can conceive, in its absence, the odor or the taste of a particular object; but none of these ideas come to us with that definiteness and perfection which mark our recollections of what we have seen. It requires, for instance, but ordinary powers of attention and perception, for a person who has one good look at a house, to recall distinctly to his mind the ideas

of its height, shape, color, material, the number of stories, the pitch of the roof, the kind of shutters to the windows, the position of the door, the fashion of panels, the bell-handle, the plate, even the little canary-bird with its cage in the windows above, and the roses, geraniums, and what else may be fairer still, in the window below. These are all objects of sight. In their absence, he can bring to mind and describe them, with almost the same accuracy that he could if they were actually present. Now, it is impossible to obtain a like precision and fulness in our conceptions of a quality which we have learned through any other sense. We form in the one case a mental image or picture of the object, which in the other case is impossible. We can by no possibility form a mental or any other image of the song of canary, of the perfume of a rose, or of any other quality, except those which address us through the eye. Our conceptions of taste, smell, touch, and even of hearing, in the absence of the objects of sense, have a certain dimness, vagueness, mistiness, uncertainty about them. The conceptions of visible objects, on the contrary, are definite, precise, and most easily recalled. Hence the knowledge derived through the sight, is, of all kinds of knowledge, the most accurate, the most easily acquired, and the most lasting.

The practical application of these views to the science of teaching, is too obvious to require more than a passing notice. Every thing which the young are to make the subject of their attention, for the purpose of remembering it, should be represented as far as possible to the eye. If the object itself, on account of its bulk, or its expensiveness, or for any other reason, cannot be exhibited for inspection, let there be some visible delineation of it by brush or pencil. If the thing to be remembered be something abstract or unreal, having neither form nor substance, perhaps it may have, or the teacher may make for it, some concrete, visible symbol, as has been done with the formulas of logic and the abstractions of arithmetic and algebra. These visible symbols on the slate and the blackboard give to those sciences all the advantages in this respect which were supposed to be peculiar to some of the branches of physical science. A boy who has forgotten every mere verbal rule both of arithmetic and algebra, will remember the formula, $x^2 + 2xy + y^2$, just as perfectly and on the same principle, as he will remember the face of the man who taught it to him. It is something which he has seen. Why has geometry in all ages been found to be of such peculiar value as a means of intellectual training? Because of the visible delineation of its doctrines by diagrams addressed to the eye. How much more readily and certainly chemical science can now be acquired, since the adoption of the present mode of symbolizing its doctrines by combinations of letters and figures. Arguments, conjectures, theories, respecting qualities addressed alike to every sense, respecting functions indeed not cognizable by any sense, are now presented on the board in visible symbolic formulas, which have the same advantage over the former mode of presenting the subject, that the sight of a chess-board during the progress of a game has over a mere verbal description of the movements.

The truth of this doctrine is strikingly illustrated in

the present mode of teaching geography, as compared with that once in use, when a child, instead of looking at the map of a country, with its boundaries and other physical characters painted to the eye, had to grope through a trackless wilderness of description. The study will be still more improved, when children shall be universally required to make as well as to look at maps, — when, to the definiteness of knowledge coming through the sight, there shall be added that inerasible impression upon the memory, which comes from fixedness and continuity of attention. It is impossible for a child to draw a map, without looking intently, and with continued attention, upon every part of that which is to be delineated. The two conditions to perfect recollection are combined, and the knowledge, which is the result, is the very last to fade from the memory.

Every teacher of small children knows how much more certainly they learn to spell by seeing than by hearing. You may repeat to a child five times over the sounds which make up a word, and he will not recollect it with half the certainty that he would on seeing it once. The same principle which leads to this result, and which indicates the propriety, not only of looking at maps but of making them, in order to the more perfect knowledge of geography, will suggest to the thoughtful teacher the expediency of children's not only looking at words, but of writing them, in order to become perfect spellers.

Mental arithmetic has its fascinations. It has, too, I am ready to admit, solid advantages. Its advantages, however, I apprehend are not precisely those which are sometimes attributed to it. There can be no doubt, I think, that it helps to cultivate the reflective powers; that it requires, and by requiring gives, the ability to confine the attention to continued mental processes. But for making expert practical accountants, which is generally quoted as its distinguishing benefit, I confess I am partial to the slate and pencil, and to that venerable parallelogram, the old-fashioned Multiplication Table, in the shape it came down to us from Pythagoras.

The reader will not, of course, understand me as wishing to discard Mental arithmetic. All that I mean to suggest is the inquiry, whether its advantages are not looked for in the wrong direction, whether they are not sometimes over-estimated, and whether this mode of teaching arithmetic, especially when pursued as a hobby, is not sometimes pushed too far, and made the means of curious display, rather than of solid and lasting benefit. In teaching mental arithmetic, too, for I would certainly teach it to some extent, I would suggest the expediency of teaching children, in performing these mental operations, to think in figures, in other words, to form conceptions of the arithmetical figures and signs, which are visible objects, rather than of quantities and relations, which are mere abstractions. Multiplication is a mere metaphysical entity. The sign of multiplication is a simple, visible symbol, addressed to the eye, and capable of being conceived by the mind with unmistakable clearness and precision. A child counting its fingers in the first steps of learning to add and to take away, is a pretty sight, doubtless. But it is painful to see a person grown to man's estate, and in other respects well educated, as I have very often seen, still dependent upon the same infantile contrivance,—still counting fingers when required to add long columns of figures. Count the fingers, if necessary, in order to get the child under way. But the sooner the leading-string can be dropped, and the child can be made to picture in his mind the pure figures and signs, their combinations and results, without reference to fingers, or apples, or cakes, or tops, the better for his arithmetic, and the better for his mental cultivation.

The subject has a painful interest for the Sabbath-School Teacher. The teacher of the infant school, indeed, has some opportunity for employing this principle of pictorial representation, in teaching the little ones of his charge. The infant school-room usually has conveniences for maps and picture cards and diagrams, and even blackboards; and most infant school teachers wisely avail themselves of the opportunity afforded. But go into the main school-room —what can the teacher do? Twenty, thirty, forty classes huddled together into one room, compact as sheep in a pen, how can the individual teacher, if disposed, use adequate visible illustrations for the instruction of his class? Where shall he place his blackboard? where shall he hang up his maps? where shall he suspend his models? where shall he exhibit his specimens? The utmost that can be done in most of our schools, as at present provided for, is to have a few maps on the distant walls of the room which the superintendent may refer to, whenever he chooses, and which all the children may see who can! The time must come, however, when the teaching of religious truth will be considered of as much importance as the teaching of arithmetic or of chemistry, and the Sabbath-School will have the same facilities for imparting instruction as the week-day school. But that time has not yet come. In the meanwhile, let the teacher carefully avail himself of whatever subsidiary aids are within his reach. No teacher should ever present himself before his class without a Bible Atlas and a Bible Dictionary in his hand. Many of those things with which his class ought to be made acquainted, are here not only described, but delineated, with equal accuracy and beauty. Thanks to the booksellers and the religious publication societies, the scenes of sacred history, and indeed religious topics generally, have been illustrated in cheap pictorial cards, both large and small, and with admirable fidelity and skill. These form a part of the indispensable furniture of the Sunday-School teacher. They are to him as necessary as are experiments, or a cabinet of specimens, to the lecturer on the physical sciences. The Sabbath-School teacher should be continually on the look-out for publications of this kind, not only for instructing and furnishing his own mind with definite ideas, but for exhibition to his class. A wise teacher will not only have something to say to his class, but also something to show. The ideas which the child gets from looking at really instructive pictures and maps, never leave him. How much also our intelligent apprehension of the scriptures is increased, by a knowledge of topography, and by associating each event in the sacred narration with the place in which it occurred?

It may be proper to say, too, in this connection, that it is with a view to the principle now under consideration, that in preparing books and papers for the young, authors and publishers feel justified in giving so much labor and space to pictorial illustration. When, indeed, such illustrations are merely for display, they deserve the contempt which they often receive. But when these pictorial illustrations have a definite meaning and design, when they teach something, when they connect in the child's mind sound religious truth with distinct and easily remembered visible forms, they are a really valuable aid in the inculcation of doctrine.

The power of attention, like all the mental powers, is by nature greater in some than in others. Still, there is no power more susceptible of improvement. The importance of its cultivation cannot well be over-stated. It affects not one study only, but all studies; not one mode of study only, but every mode of study, by text-book or by lecture; lessons to be recited by memory, or those by question and answer; not even study only, but conduct and manners, the regulation of the heart and the formation of the character. The precise measure of a child's success, in every thing that pertains to his character and standing as a scholar, will in nine cases out of ten be his power and habit of attention. There are indeed lamentable cases of wilful and intentional disorder. Yet every teacher knows that by far the greater portion of the things which interrupt and disturb a school arise from thoughtlessness and inattention. There are also equally undoubted cases of ignorance that is no crime. Yet the great majority of those who fail in their studies, fail simply because they do not attend. To attend, however, means something more than merely to be bodily present, more even than to have the ears open and the eyes fixed in the direction of the speaker, when a thing is said, or done. An old lady used to sit in the same aisle with me in church, and unfortunately lived opposite me in the street, who was neither deaf nor blind, and who was never absent from church, and yet she sent over invariably on Sunday evenings to know what it was the minister said about that meeting on Wednesday night, or that meeting on Friday night,—she did not rightly understand!

But it is not necessary to go to church, to find those who "having eyes see not, and having ears hear not, neither do they understand," who look without seeing, and hear without comprehending. Publish a notice in your school, making some change of hours or lessons, or giving any specific direction. No matter how simple, or how plainly expressed, the notice may be, or how particularly attention may be called beforehand to the announcement about to be made, where is the happy teacher who has been able on such an occasion to make himself understood by all? Teachers and preachers and speakers of every name have generally very little idea how much they are misunderstood. Let me give some instances.

In my own Sunday-School, I had neglected one morning to bring with me the teacher's class-books. After opening the school, I rang the bell as a signal for attention. There was a general hush throughout the room. All eyes were turned to the desk. I said: "Your class-books unfortunately have been left behind this morning. They have been sent for, however, and they will soon be here. As soon as they come, I will bring them round to the several classes. In the meantime, you may go on with your regular lessons." The bell was then tapped again, and the routine of the school resumed. In about a minute, a girl came up to the desk, with, "Sir, teacher says, will you please to send her class-book; it was not brought round, as usual, this morning, before school opened!" Here was a class of ten girls, averaging twelve years of age, and not one of them, nor their teacher, had heard or understood the notice which I thought I had made so plain!

Here is another instance. At the examination for admission to the Philadelphia High School, as a means of testing among other things how far this very faculty of hearing and of attention has been cultivated, the candidates are required to copy a passage from dictation. These exercises are always preserved for reference, and in order to show the fairness of the examination. On one occasion, when I was Principal of the School, I took the pains to copy out a few of the exercises, in order to show the singular freaks into which an uncultivated ear may be led. One or two specimens will serve to illustrate the point. The first clause with its variations, was as follows:—

Every	breach	of	veracity	indicates	some	latent vice.
"	bridge	"	rascality	"	"	latest vice.
"	breech	"	feracity	"	"	latinet vice.
"	preach	"	eracity	"	"	late device.
"	branch	"	vivacity	"	"	great advice.
"	"	"	veracity	"	"	late advice.
"	"	"	"	"	"	ladovice.
"	"	"	"	"	"	ladened vice.

Every branch of veracity in the next some latent vice.
Every reach of their ascidity indicates some advice.

In another part of the passage occurred the following:

Petty operations.
Petty alterations.
Petty observations.
Patriarchal occupations.
Petty oblations.

Now of what use is it to a boy who mistakes "petty" for "patriarchal," "latent vice" for "great advice," "breach of veracity" for "reach of their ascidity," who is so untrained that he really cannot hear what is said, or see what is done,—of what use is it to such a boy, merely because he has gone through a prescribed routine of books and classes, or perchance because he has attained a certain amount of years and of pounds avoirdupois, to be pushed forward into a higher department to attend lectures on chemistry, or anatomy, or morals, or history, or literature? It is preposterous. It is an insult to the Professor, and an injury to the boy.

This, then, is the burden of my song. We cannot take too much pains in early life in rousing this power of attention. Depend upon it, no matter how much learning, so called, is crammed into a youth, his intellectual development has not begun until this power is roused. He may have a vague, dreamy sort of knowledge; he may do sums by rule, and he may parse by rote, and do many other wondrous things; but his powers are not invigorated, he does not grow, until he begins really to see and hear, and feel *terra firma* under his feet.

The principle which I am illustrating applies with special force to that part of a child's education which consists in learning the meaning of words. I have serious doubts whether children ordinarily learn much of the real meaning of words by committing definitions to memory. What is a definition? It is only expressing the meaning of one word by the use of another word as nearly as possible synonymous. Now, in the case of a child, it is at least an even chance that that other word is just as unknown as the one it is intended to explain. It is like, in algebra, solving an equation with two unknown quantities, by giving the value of one unknown quantity in terms of the other. A child, for instance, is told that "potent" means "efficacious," that "power" means "ability," that "potion" means a "physical draught," that "potential" means "existing in possibility, not in act." These are definitions taken at random from a book in common use in our public schools. The definitions possibly are good enough for the purpose for which they were designed. I am not quarrelling with the definitions. But, surely, it is not by these that a child is to learn the meaning of the words. Whether he is told that "power" means "ability," or "ability" means "power," that "potent" means "efficacious, "or "efficacious" means "potent," in neither case, nine times out of ten, is any addition made to his stock of knowledge. It is not until much later in life,—until in fact our knowledge of words is already very much extended, that we profit much by learning formal definitions. But in childhood, we must learn the meaning and power of words, just as the mechanic becomes acquainted with his tools, by observing their use. A boy, for instance, reads this sentence. "The drug was very *efficacious.*" If the word is quite new to him, and there is nothing in the clause preceding or following to indicate its meaning, it is not at all unlikely that he may suppose it to mean "poisonous." If, however, from the context, he finds that a person who had been sick, was made suddenly well, and this statement followed by the remark, that "the drug was very *efficacious,*" he will probably get the idea that the word means "healing," or "curative." He reads again, in another place, that a certain mode of teaching penmanship was found to be very "efficacious." Here is a new use of the word, quite different from the other, and he is obliged to exclude from his idea of its meaning every thing like "healing." So he goes on, every fresh example cutting off some extraneous idea which the previous examples had led him to attach to the word, and every step onward coming nearer to the general idea, though he may never express it in words, of something which accomplished its object, whatever that object may be. It is, I believe, chiefly by observing in this way the manner in which words are used, that children do and must learn their meaning. It is, in other words, by quickening and cultivating the habit of attention to the meaning,—by training a child, when he is reading, to imagine, not that he is reading the words, but that he is reading the sense, by accustoming him to look through the word, to the sense, just as he would look at objects out of doors through the window, and to consider the words, as he would consider the glass, merely as a medium, through which, and unmindful of it, he looks at something beyond,—*which something is the meaning.*

Let me not be misunderstood in regard to this matter of definitions. I believe it to be of the utmost importance that children should be constantly required to give definitions or explanations of the words whose meaning they have acquired. All I mean to call in question is, whether that meaning to any considerable extent is acquired by committing to memory formal definitions prepared by others. When they have once learned the meaning of a word, which is to be done mainly, if not only, by observing its use, then by all means let them be required to express that meaning by other words which they know. Such an exercise cannot be too much insisted on. It is one of the best means of securing that attention to the signification of words, which is so much wanted. It requires the child, moreover, to bring his knowledge continually to the test. It cultivates at once accuracy of thought, and accuracy of language, which is the vehicle of thought. Train a child, therefore, to the habit of attention, first to the meaning of words as gathered from observation of their use, and secondly to the expression of that meaning in language appropriate and intelligible to others.

I have dwelt a little on this subject, because, as in the matter of hearing, I doubt whether people generally are aware how little children understand what they read. Nor is this ignorance confined to children. In our acts of devotion, we are all in the habit of using certain stereotyped phrases, without attaching to them any definite meaning, without perhaps so much as having even thought whether they had a meaning. This same pernicious habit is seen also in our reading of the Scriptures. We have read the phrases over from childhood, until we have become so familiar with them, that we are obliged often to stop, and by a sort of compulsory process to challenge each word as it passes, and see whether it really conveys any meaning to our mind.

If I were to say to a class, "The Bible tells us of a man who was older than his father," or some such apparent contradiction in terms, the sharp antithesis would doubtless arrest their attention, and I would at least be asked to explain myself. Yet, ten to one, they have read, hundreds of times, of him who is "the *root* and the *offspring* of David, the bright and morning star," without noticing anything at all remarkable in the expression. It is to them merely something good and pious, couched in a very pleasant and sonorous flow of words, and meaning doubtless something very comforting and edifying.

I was once teaching temporarily a young ladies' Bible Class. The average age of the members was at least seventeen. They were the pick from a large city school, and had been selected for their superior educational advantages and attainments. Most of them were attending expensive private schools during the week. Wishing to satisfy myself as to the general knowledge and the intellectual habits of the members, I took the plan of simply reading verse about, stopping from time to time to talk familiarly about anything which might happen to suggest itself. This verse among others was read: it is from the account of the miracle on the day of Pentecost: "And there appeared unto them cloven tongues like as of fire, and it sat upon each of them." I found, upon inquiring, that *not one* in that large class had the remotest idea of what was meant by the word "cloven." One young lady thought it meant "fiery," another "flaming," another "winged," and so on. Most of them, however, said that they really had never thought of the matter before. Probably every one of them had read the passage hundreds of times; and when we began talking about it, no one of them seemed to have an idea that there was anything in the verse which she did not understand. It was not until I took it up, word by word, and challenged a peremptory and sharp scrutiny into the meaning attached to each word, that the remarkable fact came out which I have stated.

One or two more leaves from my professional experience will be given.

During the greater part of my professional life, it has been a part of my duty to examine candidates for the office of teacher in the public schools. Out of ninety-eight candidates for the office of assistant teacher, whom I examined on one occasion, only one knew the meaning of the word "sumptuary," although in the public discussion then going on about the license law, the word was in daily use in the public papers; in fact, I took it out of the newspaper of that morning. On another occasion, out of fourteen candidates for the office of Principal teacher of a boys' Grammar school, four defined "friable" as that which can be fried; several did not know at all the meaning of "hibernating," and one, the successful candidate, said it meant "relating to Ireland." By "successful" candidate, I mean the one who got the vote of the Directors!

This sober scrutiny into any one's knowledge of the meaning of words in common use, is one of the most reliable tests of his general intellectual progress and cultivation. It is one of the means by which in many city schools it is customary to test a candidate's fitness for promotion. To show how little people generally, and even teachers, are aware of the extent to which children misconceive the meaning of words in common use, I have transcribed a few examples from an examination of the kind which I once held. The definitions which I am about to quote were not the work of oral confusion and haste, but were given in writing, in circumstances of entire quietude and ample deliberation. The average age of the candidates, on the occasion referred to, was fourteen years and ten months, and no one of them was by law under thirteen years.

Stature—A picture; "I saw a stature of Washington."

Fabulous—Full of threads; "Silk is fabulous."

Accession—The act of eating a great deal; "John got very sick after dinner by accession."

Atonement—A small insect; "Queen Mab was pulled by little atonements." Sound, [orthodox]; "They went to the church of the Atonement."

Auxiliary—To form; "The gardener did auxiliary his garden."

Ingredient—A native-born; "Tobacco is an ingredient of this country."

Fragment—Sweetmeats; "It was a fragment."

Develop—To swallow up; "God sent a whale to develop Jonah."

Exotic—Relating to a government; "Some countries have a very exotic government." Patriotic; "He was exotic in the cause of Independence." Absolute; "The government of Turkey is exotic." Standing out; "The company were exotic."

Circumference—Distance through the middle. Distance around the middle of the outside.

Callous—Something which cannot be effected; "That America should gain her independence was supposed to be callous."

Mobility—Belonging to the people; "The mobility of St. Louis has greatly increased."

Anomalous—Powerful; "His speech was considered anomalous."

Adequate—A land animal; "An elephant is an adequate."

Transition—The act of transcribing; "The transition of that book was gaining ground in the public mind."

Gregarious—Pertaining to idols; "The Sandwich Islands worship gregarious." Pertaining to an oak; "The Druids were noted for their gregarious exercises." Consisting of grain. Grass-eating. Full of talk. Full of color.

Propensity—Dislike; "He had a propensity to study."

Artificially—Belonging to flowers.

Fluctuation—coming in great numbers; "There was a great fluctuation of emigrants." Setting on fire. Beating.

Odium—That you have a great tact at anything; "Your odium is very great." A poisonous herb.

Pertaining to song; "He was an odium writer." A sweet smell; "The odium of new-mown hay."

Transverse — To turn over; "Transverse that bucket and see what is in it." To change from verse; "Some writers change books from transverse to verse." To verse again; "He transversed his copy." To spread abroad; "They transverse the Bible."

Utility — Relating to the soil; "The ground it remarkable for its utility."

Quadruple — Relating to birds; "There was a number of quadruple."

Alternate — Not ternate.

Menace — A tare in the flesh; "The dog caused a menace in John's arm."

Vital — Relating to death; "Vital spark of heavenly flame."

Intrinsic — not trinsic. Weak, feeble; "He was a very intrinsic old man."

Subservient — One opposed to the upholding of servants. Stubborn; "On account of the boy being subservient he was turned out of school."

Perfidy — Trust; not to cheat; "Such a man is perfidy; that is, everything can be trusted to him." Accessible; "Some persons have a great deal of perfidy."

Access — Intermission; "Joseph had access of his teacher to go into the room."

Vicinity — In the same direction; "Pekin is in the vicinity of Philadelphia."

Subsequent — Preceding; "The subsequent chapter."

Infectious — To make fectious.

Exquisite — To be in a quisitive manner. To help. To find out. Talkative. Not required.

Mingle — To tear in pieces.

Deride — To ride down.

Manifold — Made by the hand. Pertaining to man; "Forgive our manifold sins."

I have failed entirely in the general drift of this chapter, if I have not made it obvious that the principle which I have been attempting to illustrate is one of singularly pervading influence, and of most various and manifold applications. The subject is indeed eminently suggestive. One single additional line of illustration, however, must suffice. I refer to the application of this principle to what may be called the incidentals of teaching and training..

A child, for instance, should not only "spell out of book," as it is called, but his attention should by some means be directed to the way in which words are spelled. He should be accustomed to form, as it were, a mental image of each word, to think of it as having a particular form and appearance, so that his eye will detect instantly a wanting or an excrescent letter, just as he sees a wen, a defective limb, or a distorted feature on the person of an acquaintance. Only fire his young ambition with the aim to spell well, and quicken his attention to the way in which words are spelled, and every time he reads a book he receives incidentally a lesson in spelling.

A child should have stated exercises and systematic instructions in the art of reading. But quite as much improvement in this important and too much neglected accomplishment may be gained by not allowing children at any time to read in an improper manner. Every demonstration at the blackboard, every text or hymn repeated from memory, every recitation in arithmetic, grammar, or geography, every exercise of every kind in which the voice is used and words are uttered, may be made an incidental lesson in reading. By being never allowed to pronounce words incorrectly, to utter them in a low or drawling manner, or to crowd and overlap them, as it were, one upon the other, the ear becomes accustomed to the correct sounds of the language, and immediately detects any variation from its accustomed standard. By thus insisting, in every vocal exercise, upon the full and correct pronunciation of the elementary sounds of the language, more may be done to make good readers and speakers than by all the pronouncing dictionaries and elocution books in print.

Let a child by all means take lessons in writing. Let him learn plain text, German text, round hand, running hand, back hand, and the flourishes. But if he is to become rapidly master of that truly beautiful and most useful accomplishment, let the teacher insist upon his always attending to his manner of writing, and always writing as well as he can. Whether he writes a composition, a sketch, a letter, whenever for any purpose he puts pen to paper, let him be required to form each letter distinctly, to write it gracefully, and to give to his exercise a neat and elegant appearance. Teach him to think of a crooked line or a blotted page as of an untied shoe, or a dirty face. By thus making every written exercise an exercise in writing, his progress will be increased beyond your expectations, and you will soon see him looking with pleasure at the clean and symmetrical forms which flow so gracefully from his pen, as he goes from line to line over the virgin page, no half-formed or misshapen letters to embarrass, but all in every part as elegantly written as it is easily read.

Grammar should no doubt be taught by text-book and in stated lessons. The parts of speech, the conjugations and declensions, syntax and parsing, must all be systematically conned, the rules and definitions committed to memory, and the judgment exercised upon their application. At the same time every recitation of a child, as well as all his conversation, ought to be made an incidental and unconscious lesson in grammar. Only never allow him to use unchallenged an incorrect or ungrammatical expression, train his ear to detect and revolt at it, as at a discordant note in music, let him if possible hear nothing but sterling, honest English, and he will then learn grammar to some purpose. If, on the contrary, he is allowed to recite and to talk in whatever language comes uppermost, and to hear continually those around him reciting and talking in a similar manner, he may parse till he is blind without learning "to speak and write the English language correctly." Banish from the nursery, the school-room, and the play-ground, incorrect and ungrammatical expressions, and you do more than can be done in all other ways to preserve "the well of English undefiled."

Young persons need systematic instructions in the principles which should govern their conduct. They need not indeed be troubled with the more abstruse questions in the theory of morals. But the great obvious rules of duty should be taught them, in a systematic manner, by a competent instructor. But that man would be thought little acquainted with the influences which go to mould and form the character, who should suppose the matter ended here. The doctrines inculcated in the lesson, must be carried out and applied in all the petty incidents of the day. Not an hour passes in a large family or a school, without an occurrence involving some principle in morals. A boy of moderate talents, notwithstanding all his exertions, is eclipsed by one more gifted, and he is tempted to envy. Imagining himself aggrieved or insulted by his fellows, he burns for revenge. Overtaken in a fault and threatened with punishment, he is tempted to lie. Misled by the opinion of others, or esteeming some rule of his teachers harsh and unnecessary, he is inclined to disobey. These and a hundred other instances which might be named, will suggest to the thoughtful parent or teacher so many opportunities for giving incidentally the most important practical instruction in morals.

In these and the manifold other illustrations which might be given, the essential point is to quicken and keep alive the attention. Whatever be the subject of study, and whether the instructions be direct or incidental, let children be preserved from attending to it in a sluggish, listless, indifferent manner. The subject of study, in the case of young persons, is often of less importance than the manner of study. I have been led sometimes to doubt the value of many of the inventions for facilitating the acquisition of knowledge by children. That knowledge the acquisition of which costs no labor, will not be likely to make a deep impression, or to remain long upon the memory. It is by labor that the mind strengthens and grows: and while care should be taken not to overtask it by exertions beyond its strength, yet let it never be forgotten that mere occupation of the mind, even with useful and proper objects, is not the precise aim of education. The educator aims, not to make learned boys, but able men. To do this, he must tax their powers. He must rouse them to manly exertion. He must teach them to think, to discriminate, to digest what they have received, to work. Every day there must be the glow of hard work,— not the exhaustion and languor which arise from too protracted confinement to study,— which have the same debilitating effect upon the mind that a similar process has upon the body,— but vigorous and hardy labor, such as wakens the mind from its lethargy, summons up the resolution and the will, and puts the whole internal man into a state of determined and positive activity. The boy in such a case feels that he is at work. He feels, too, that he is gaining something more than knowledge. He is gaining power. He is growing in strength. He grapples successfully to-day with a difficulty that would have staggered him yesterday. There is no mistaking this process; and no matter what the subject of study, the intellectual development what it gives, is worth infinitely more than all that vague, floating kind of knowledge sometimes sought after, which seems to be imbibed somehow from the atmosphere of the school-room, as it certainly evaporates the moment a boy enters the atmosphere of men and of active life.

XXVII.

GAINING THE ATTENTION.

THE teacher who fails to get the attention of his scholars, fails totally. The pupils may perhaps learn something, because they may give the lesson some study at home, under the direction of their parents. But they learn nothing from the teacher. He is really no teacher, though he may occupy the teacher's seat. There is, and there can be, no teaching, where the attention of the scholar is not secured. Gaining the attention is an indispensable condition to the thing called teaching. Not, however, the only indispensable thing. We have seen a class wrought by special tricks and devices to the highest pitch of excited attention,—fairly panting with eagerness, all eyes and ears, on the very tiptoe of aroused mental activity,—yet learning nothing. The teacher had the knack of stirring them up and lashing them into a half frenzy of excited expectation, without having any substantial knowledge wherewith to reward their eagerness. With all his one-sided skill, he was but a mountebank. To real, successful teaching, there must be these two things, namely, the ability to hold the minds of the children, and the ability to pour into the minds thus presented sound and seasonable instruction. Lacking the latter ability, your pupil goes away with his vessel unfilled. Lacking the former, you only pour water upon the ground.

How shall the teacher secure attention?

In the first place, let him make up his mind that he will have it. This is half the battle. Let him settle it with himself, that until he does this, he is doing nothing; that without the attention of his scholars, he is no more a teacher, than is the chair he occupies. If he is not plus, he is zero, if not actually minus. With this truth fully realized, he will come before his class resolved to have a hearing; and this very resolution, written as it will be all over him, will have its effect upon his scholars. Children are quick to discern the mental attitude of a teacher. They know, as if by instinct, whether he is in earnest or not, and in all ordinary cases they yield without dispute to a claim thus resolutely put.

This, then, is the first duty of the teacher in this matter. He must go to his class with the resolute determination of making every scholar feel his presence all the time. The moment any scholar shows that the consciousness of his teacher's presence is not on his mind, as a restraining power, something is wrong. The first step towards producing that consciousness, as an abiding influence on the minds of the scholars, is for the teacher to determine in his own mind and bring it about. Without being arrogant, without being dictatorial, without being or doing anything that is disagreeable or unbecoming, he must yet make up his mind to put forth in the class a distinct power of self-assertion. He must determine to make them feel that he is there, that he is there all the time, that he is there to every one of them.

In the next place, the teacher must not disappoint the attention which his manner has challenged. He must have something valuable to communicate to the expectant minds before him. He must be thoroughly prepared in the lesson, so that the pupils shall feel that they are learning from him. His lips must keep knowledge. The human heart thirsts for knowledge. This is one of its natural instincts. It is indeed often much perverted, and many are to be found who even show aversion to being instructed. Yet the normal condition of things is otherwise, and nothing is more common than to see children hanging with fondness around any one who has something to tell them. Let the teacher then be sure to have something to say, as well as determined to say it.

In the third place, the teacher must have his knowledge perfectly at command. It must be on the tip of his tongue. If he hesitates, and stops to think, or to look in his book for the purpose of hunting up what he has to tell them, he will be very apt to lose his chance. Teaching children, particularly young children, is like shooting birds on the wing. The moment your bird is in sight, you must fire. The moment you have the child's eye, be ready to speak. This readiness of utterance is a matter to be cultivated. The ripest scholars are often sadly deficient in it. The very habit of profound study is apt to induce the opposite quality to readiness. A teacher who is conscious of this defect, must resolutely set himself to resist it and overcome it. He can do so, if he will. But it requires resolution and practice.

In the fourth place, the teacher must place himself so that every pupil in the class is within the range of his vision. It is not uncommon to see a teacher pressing close up to the scholars in the centre of the class, so that those at the right and left ends are out of his sight; or if he turns his face to those on one side, he at the same time turns his back to those on the other. Always sit or stand where you can all the while see the face of every pupil. I have, hundreds of times, seen the whole character of the instruction and discipline of a class changed by the observance of this simple rule.

Another rule is to use your eyes quite as much as your tongue. If you want your class to look at you, you must look at them. The eye has a magic power. It wins, it fascinates, it guides, it rewards, it punishes, it controls. You must learn how to see every child all the time. Some teachers seem to be able to see only one scholar at a time. This will never do. While you are giving this absorbed, undivided attention to one, all the rest are running wild. Neither will it do for the teacher to be looking about much, to see what is going on among the other classes in the room. Your scholars' eyes will be very apt to follow yours. You are the engineer, they are the passengers. If you run off the track, they must do likewise. Nor must your eye be occupied with the book, hunting up question and answer, nor dropped to the floor in excessive modesty. All the power of seeing that you have is needed for looking earnestly, lovingly, without interruption, into the faces and eyes of your pupils.

But for the observance of this rule, another is indispensable. You must learn to teach without book. Perhaps you cannot do this absolutely. But the nearer you can approach to it, the better. Thorough preparation, of course, is the secret of this power. Some teachers think they have prepared a lesson when they have gone over it once, and studied out all the answers. There could not be a greater mistake. This is only the first step in the preparation. You might as well think that you have learned the Multiplication Table, and are prepared to teach it, when you have gone over it once and seen by actual count that the figures are all right, and you know where to put your finger on them when required. You are prepared to teach a lesson when you have all the facts and ideas in it at your tongue's end, so that you can go through them all, in proper order, without once referring to the book. Any preparation short of this will not do, if you want to command attention. Once prepare a lesson in this way, and it will give you such freedom in the art of teaching, and you will experience such a pleasure in it, that you will never want to relapse into the old indolent habit.

XXVIII.

COUNSELS.

1. *To a Young Teacher.*

YOU are about to assume the charge of a class in the school under my care. Allow me, in a spirit of frankness, to make to you a brief statement of some of the aims of the institution, and of the principles by which we are guided in their prosecution.

1. "Unless the Lord build the house, they labor in vain that build it." I have no professional conviction more fixed and abiding than this, that no persons more need the direct, special, continual guidance of the Holy Spirit than those who undertake to mould and discipline the youthful mind. No preparation for this office is complete which does not include devout prayer for that wisdom which cometh from above. If any one possession, more than another, is the direct gift of the Almighty, it would seem to be that of knowledge. The teacher, therefore, of all men, is called upon to look upwards to a source that is higher than himself. He needs light in his own mind; he should not count it misspent labor to ask for light to be given to the minds of his scholars. There is a Teacher infinitely

wiser and more skilful than any human teacher. The instructor must be strangely blind to the resources of his profession, who fails to resort habitually to that great, plenary, unbounded source of light and knowledge. While, therefore, we aim in this school to profit by all subsidiary and subordinate methods and improvements in the art of teaching, we first of all seek the aid of our Heavenly Father; we ask wisdom of Him who "giveth liberally and upbraideth not." This, then, is the first principle that governs us in the work here assigned us. The fear of God is the beginning of knowledge. We who are teachers endeavor to show that we ourselves fear God, and we inculcate the fear of Him as the first and highest duty of our scholars; and in every plan and effort to guide the young minds committed to us, we ourselves look for guidance to the only unerring source of light.

2. In proportion to the implicitness with which we rely upon divine aid, should be the diligence with which we use all the human means within our reach. It should therefore, in the second place, be the aim of the teachers of this school to acquaint themselves diligently with the most approved methods of teaching. No teachers will be retained who do not keep themselves well posted in the literature of their profession, and who are not found continually aiming at self-improvement. In whatever school of whatever country, any branch is taught by better methods than those practised here, it should be the duty of a teacher in this school to search it out, and to profit by the discovery. Improvement comes by comparison. The man, or the institution, that fails to profit by the experience

of others, is not wise. I hold it to be the duty of every teacher of this school to be habitually conversant with the educational journals of the day, and with the standard works on the theory of teaching, and to lose no opportunity for personal observation of the methods of others. I have often noticed, with equal pain and commiseration, that young teachers, after having once finished their preliminary studies and obtained a situation, are thereupon apparently quite content, making no further effort at improvement, but settling down for life in an inglorious mediocrity. The best teachers in this school are expected to be better teachers next year than they are now,—with ampler stores of knowledge, and a happier faculty for communicating it. This, then, is our second aim in this school. We aim to have teachers thoroughly posted in regard to the theory and the methods of teaching, prepared to ride upon the advance wave of every real improvement in the art.

3. I should, however, fail entirely to convey my meaning, were I to lead you to suppose that we expect to accomplish our ends mainly by fine-spun theories. I have no faith in any theory of education, which does not include, as one of its leading elements, *hard work*. The teachers of this school expect to work hard, and we expect the scholars to work hard. We have no royal road to learning. Any knowledge, the acquisition of which costs nothing, is usually worth nothing. The mind, equally with the body, grows by labor. If some stuffing process could be invented, by which knowledge could be forced into a mind perfectly passive, the knowledge so acquired would be worthless to

its possessor, and would soon pass away, leaving the mind as blank as it was before. Knowledge, to be of any value, must be assimilated, as bodily food is. Teaching is essentially a co-operative act. The mind of the teacher and the mind of the scholar must both act, and must act together, in intellectual co-operation and sympathy, if there is to be any true mental growth. Teaching is not merely hearing lessons. It is not mere talking. It is something more than mere telling. It is causing a child to know. It is awakening attention, and then satisfying it. It is an out-and-out live process. The moment the mind of the teacher or the mind of the scholar flags, real teaching ceases. This, then, is our third aim. We aim in this school to accomplish results, not by fanciful theories, but by *bona fide* hard work,— by keeping teachers and scholars, while at their studies, wide awake and full of life; not by exhausting drudgery, nor by fitful, irregular, spasmodic exertions, but by steady, persevering, animated, straightforward work.

4. A fourth aim which we have steadily before us, is to make *thorough* work of whatever acquisition we attempt. A little knowledge, well learned and truly digested, and made a part of the pupil's own intellectual stores, is worth more to him than any amount of facts loosely and indiscriminately brought together. In intellectual, as in other tillage, the true secret of thrift is to plough deep, not to skim over a large surface. The prevailing tendency at this time, in systems of education, is unduly to multiply studies. So many new sciences are being brought within the pale of popular knowledge, that it is no longer possible,

in a school like this, to embrace within its course of study all the subjects which it is practicable and desirable for people generally to know. Through the whole encyclopædia of arts and sciences, there is hardly one which has not its advocates, and which has not strong claims to recognition. The teacher is simply infatuated who attempts to embrace them all in his curriculum. He thereby puts himself under an absolute necessity of being superficial, and he generates in his scholars pretension and conceit. Old James Ross, the grammarian, famous as a teacher in Philadelphia more than half a century ago, had on his sign simply these words, "Greek and Latin taught here." Assuredly I would not advocate quite so rigid an exclusion as that, nor, if limited to only two studies, would it be those. But I have often thought Mr. Ross's advertisement suggestive. Better even that extreme than the encyclopædic system which figures so largely on some circulars. Mr. Ross indeed taught nothing but Latin and Greek. But he taught these languages better probably than they have ever been taught on this continent; and any two branches thoroughly mastered are of more service to the pupil than twenty branches known imperfectly and superficially. A limited field, then, and thorough work. This is our fourth aim.

5. As a fifth aim, we endeavor, in the selection of subjects of study, not to allow the common English branches, as they are called, to be shoved aside. To read well, to write a good hand, to be expert in arithmetic, to have such a knowledge of geography and history as to read intelligently what is going on and the world, to have such a

knowledge of one's own language as to use it correctly and purely in speaking and composition,—these are attainments to be postponed to no others. These are points of primary importance, to be aimed at by every one, whatever else he may omit.

6. We aim, in the sixth place, to mark the successive parts of the course of study by well defined limits. There are in the course of study successive stages of progress, and these stages are made as clear and precise as it is possible to make them; and no pupil is allowed to go forward until the ground behind is thoroughly mastered. At the same time, these stages in study should be kept all the while before the minds of the pupils as goals to be aimed at. There are, for this purpose, at briefly recurring intervals, examinations for promotion. While no pupil is permitted to go forward, except as the result of a rigorous examination, the idea of an advance should, if possible, never be allowed to be absent from his thoughts. That scholar should be counted worthy of highest honor, not who stands highest in a particular room, but who by successful examinations can pass most rapidly from room to room. That teacher is considered most successful, not who retains most pupils, but who in a given time pushes most pupils forward into a higher room. We want no scholar to stand still for a single week. Motion, progress, definite achievement, must be the order of the day.

7. We aim, in the seventh place, to cultivate in every pupil a habit of attention and observation. Youth is the time when the senses should be most assiduously trained. The young should be taught to see for themselves, to

ascertain the qualities of objects by the use of their own eyes and hands, to notice whether a thing is distant and how far distant it is, whether it is heavy and how heavy, whether it has color and what color, whether it has form and what form. They should learn to study real things by actually noticing them with their own senses, and then learning to apply the right words to the knowledge so acquired. We aim to apply this habit of observation in all the branches of study, so that in every stage of progress the scholar shall know, not merely the names of things, but the things themselves. In other words, we would cultivate real, as well as verbal knowledge, and aim to awaken in every pupil an active, inquiring, observant state of mind.

---

2. *To a New Pupil.*

You have just been admitted to the privileges of this institution, and are about to enter here upon a course of study. The occasion is one eminently suited for serious reflection. At the close of a school career it is difficult not to reflect. Thoughts upon one's course will, at such a time, force themselves upon us. But then it is too late. The good we might have achieved, is beyond our grasp, and its contemplation is profitable only as a legitimate topic of contrition. How much wiser and more profitable to anticipate the serious judgment which sooner or later we must pass upon our actions, and so to shape our conduct in advance, that the retrospect, when it comes, may be a source of joy and congratulation, rather than of shame and repentance. How much wiser to direct our bark to some definite and well selected channel, than to float at random along the current of events, the sport of every idle wave. Men are divided into two classes,—those who control their own destiny, doing what they mean to do, living according to a plan which they prefer and prepare, and those who are controlled by circumstances, who have a vague purpose of doing something or being somebody in the world, but leave the means to chance. The season of youth generally determines to which of these classes you will ultimately belong. It is here, at school, that you decide whether, when you come to man's estate, you will be a governing man, or whether you will be a mere aimless driveller. Those who at the beginning of a course in school make to themselves a distinct aim, towards which day after day they work their course, undiscouraged by defeat, unseduced by ease or the temptation of a temporary pleasure, not only win the immediate objects of pursuit, but gain for themselves those habits of aiming, of perseverance, of self-control, which will make them hereafter controlling and governing men. Those, on the contrary, who enter upon an academic career with an indefinite purpose of studying after a fashion, whenever it is not too hot, or too cold, or the lessons are not too hard, or there is nothing special going on to distract the attention, or who are content to swim along lazily with the multitude, trusting to the good-nature of the teacher, to an occasional deception, or to the general chapter of accidents, for escape from censure, and for such an amount of proficiency as on the whole will pass muster with friends or the public,—depend upon it, such youths are doomed, inevitably doomed, all their days, to be nobodies, or worse.

Let me, then, my young friend, as preliminary to your entering upon the duties before you, call to your mind some of those things, which, as an intelligent and responsible being, you should deliberately aim to follow or to avoid while in this school. In the counsels which I am going to give you, I shall make no attempt to say what is new or striking. My aim will be rather to recall to your memory some few of those familiar maxims, in which you have been, I dare say, often instructed elsewhere.

1. First of all, remember that men always, by a necessary law, fall below the point at which they aim. You well understand that if a projectile be hurled in the direct line of any elevated object, the force of gravity will cause the projectile to deflect from the line of direction, and this deflection and curvature will be great in proportion to the distance of the object to be reached. Hence, in gunnery, the skilful marksman invariably takes aim above the point which he expects to hit. At certain distances, he will aim 45° above the horizon at what is really but 30° above it. So, in moral subjects, there is unfortunately a native and universal tendency downwards, which deflects us out of the line in which good resolutions would propel us. You aim to be distinguished, and you turn out only meritorious. You aim to be meritorious, and you fall into the multitude. You are content with being of the multitude, and you fall out of your class entirely. So also, as in physical projectiles, the extent of your departure from the right line is measured by the distance of the objects

at which you aim. You resolve to avoid absolutely and entirely certain practices for a day or a week, and you can perhaps keep very close to the mark. But who can hold himself up to an exact fulfilment of his intentions for a whole term? I do not wish to discourage you. The drift of my argument is, not that you should make no aim, but that you should fix your aim *high*, and that you should then keep yourself up to your good resolutions, as long and as closely as you possibly can.

2. In the next place, remember that no excellence is ever attained without self-denial. Wisdom's ways are indeed ways of pleasantness. The satisfaction of having done well and nobly is of a certain ravishing kind, far surpassing other enjoyments. But to obtain this high and satisfying pleasure, many minor and incompatible pleasures must be foregone. You cannot have the pleasure of being a first-rate scholar, and at the same time have your full swing of fun. I am not opposed to fun. I like it myself. No one enjoys it more. Nor do I think the exercise and enjoyment of it incompatible with the highest scholastic excellence. But there is a place for all things, and school is not the place for fun. If you enjoy in moderation out of school the relaxation and refreshment which jokes, wit, and pleasantry give, you will be all the more likely to grapple successfully with the serious employments which await you here. Still do not forget that your employments here are serious. Study is a sober business. If you would acquire really useful knowledge, you must be willing to work. You must make up your mind to say "no" to the thousand opportunities and temptations to frivolous behavior

that will beset you in school. You must not be content with being studious and orderly merely when the eye of authority is upon you. This is to be simply an eye-servant and a hypocrite. To have a little pleasantry in the school-room, to perpetrate or to join in some witty practical joke, may seem to you comparatively harmless. So it would be but for its expense. You buy it at the cost of benefits which no money can measure, and no future time can replace. There are seasons of the year when the farmer may indulge in relaxation,— may go abroad on excursions of pleasure, or may saunter away the time in comparative idleness at home. But in the few precious weeks of seedtime, every day, every hour is of moment. This is your seedtime. Every hour of school-time that you waste in trifling is an injury and a loss to your future. Remember, then, that you cannot reach high excellence in school, or that pure and noble enjoyment, which is its exceeding great reward, without self-denial. Resolve, therefore, here and now, steadfastly, immovably, to say "no" to everything in school, no matter how innocent in itself, which shall interfere with the progress of study for a single moment. If you make such a fixed resolution, and live up to it, you will soon be surprised to find how easy and pleasant the discipline of school has become.

3. Among the mischievous fallacies of young persons at school, I know none that work more to their own disadvantage than the opinion that a particular teacher is prejudiced against them. Against this feeling it seems impossible to reason. When once scholars have it fairly in their heads that a certain teacher is partial, in whatever

relates to their standing, I have been almost forced to the conclusion that it is best not to attempt reasoning with them. Under such feelings, indeed, by a singular freak of human nature, scholars are often driven to do, in sheer bravado or defiance, the very things which they imagine to be unjustly imputed to them. Allow me, my young friend, to ask you candidly and in all seriousness to turn this matter over in your own mind. What adequate motive can you imagine for a teacher's marking you otherwise than impartially? Every teacher has an interest in having as many high marks and as few demerits under his signature as possible. It is not to his credit that he should be unable to maintain order without blackening his roll with bad marks. A class roll filled with 0's is not the kind of evidence a teacher covets as to his skill in teaching. Notice the intercourse between the teachers and those scholars who are admitted on all hands to be strictly and conscientiously correct in their behavior. See what a pleasure it affords the instructor to have to deal with such pupils. See what a satisfaction the teacher experiences when, at the close of the day, there is not a demerit mark on his book. Judge, then, whether it is not likely to be a self-denial and a cross to him, when a sense of duty compels him to do otherwise. Be slow, therefore, to impute bad marks to injustice, or ill nature. No man of course is infallible, and teachers make mistakes as well as other people. But the temptations to do intentional wrong are, in this case, all the other way.

4. Closely connected with the habit just mentioned is the disposition to neglect particular branches of study.

From disliking a teacher, the transition is easy to a dislike for his department. Others again, without any personal feeling in the case, think that they have a natural fitness for one class of studies, and an equally natural *un*-fitness for another class. So they content themselves with proficiency in that in which they already excel, and neglect that in which they are deficient, and which therefore they find difficult. Is this wise? The branches which you find difficult, are precisely those in which you need an instructor. Besides, the object of education is to develop equally and harmoniously all your faculties. If the memory, the reasoning faculty, the imagination, or any one power of the mind, is active far beyond the other powers, that surely is no reason for giving additional stimulus and growth in that direction. On the contrary, bend your main energies towards bringing forward your other faculties to an equal development. If you have a natural or acquired preference for mathematics, and a dislike for languages, the former study will take care of itself: bend all your energies to the latter. So, if languages are your choice, and mathematical study your aversion, take hold of the odious task with steady and sturdy endeavor, and you will soon convert it into a pleasure. The same is true of grammar, of geography, of history, of composition, of rhetoric, of mental and moral science, of elocution,— of every branch. If you are wise, you will give your chief attention in school to those branches for which you feel the least inclination, and in which you find it most difficult to excel. You should do so, because, in the first place, this failure and disinclination, in nine cases out of ten, grow out of defective training heretofore, and not from any defect in your mental constitution; and, secondly, if your natural constitution should be, as in some cases it is, one-sided and exceptional, your aim should be to correct and cure, not to aggravate, the defects of nature. This advice, you will observe, relates to your course in school, not to your choice of a profession in life. When your career in school is finished, and you are about to select a profession, follow by all means the bent of your genius. Do that for which you have the greatest natural or acquired aptitude. But here, the case is different. Your aim in school is to develop your powers,—to grow into an accomplished and capable man,—to acquire complete command of all the mental resources God has given you.

5. There is a practice, common to school-life everywhere, known by the not very dignified name of cheating. There is, I fear, among young people generally, while at school, an erroneous and mischievous state of opinion on this subject. Deception in regard to your lessons is not viewed, as it should be, in the light of a serious moral delinquency. An ingenuous youth, who would scorn to steal, and scorn to lie anywhere else than at school, makes no scruple to deceive a teacher. Is honesty a thing of place and time? I do not say, I would not trust at my money-drawer the boy who has been cheating at his lessons, because a boy may have been led into the latter delinquency by a false notion of right, which as yet has not affected his integrity in matters of business. But this I do say. Cheating at school blunts the moral sense; it impairs the sense of personal honor; it breaks down the outworks of integrity;

it leads by direct and easy steps to that grosser cheating which ends in the penitentiary.

On this subject, I once had a most painful experience. A boy left school with as fair a character for honesty as many others against whom nothing can be said except that they do sometimes practise deceit in regard to their lessons. I really believed him to be an honest boy, and recommended him as such. By means of the recommendation, he obtained in a large store a responsible post connected with the receipt and payment of money. His employer was pleased with his abilities, and disposed to give him rapid promotion. After a few months, I inquired after him, and found that he had been detected in forcing his balances! I do verily believe, the dishonest purpose, which led to this pecuniary fraud, grew directly out of a facility at deception acquired at school. He had cheated his teacher; he had cheated his father; he had obtained a fictitious average; he had gained a standing and credit in school not justly his due; why should he not exercise the same ingenuity in improving his pecuniary resources?

Independently of the moral effect of these deceptive practices upon your own character, is there not in the acts themselves an inherent meanness and baseness, from which a pure-minded youth would instinctively recoil? Is there not something false and rotten in the prevailing sentiment on this subject among young persons at school? When by some convenient fiction you reach a higher standard than your merits entitle you to, is it not so far forth at the expense of some more conscientious competitor? And, after all, when you deceive a teacher into the belief that you are studying when you are not, that you know a thing when you do not know it, that you wrote a composition, or executed a drawing, which was done by some one else, —whom do you cheat but yourself? You may deceive the teacher, but the loss is yours.

6. If there could be such a thing as an innocent crime, I would say it was that of talking in school. There can hardly be named a more signal instance of an act so perfectly innocent in itself, becoming so seriously blameworthy purely and solely by circumstances. I believe I express the common opinion of all who have had any experience in the matter, when I say that three fourths of all the intentional disorder, and at least nine tenths of all the actual interruptions to study, grow out of the practice of unlicensed talking. And yet this is the very last thing which young persons will admit into their serious, practical convictions as being an evil and a wrong. They may admit that they get bad marks by it; that it brings them into trouble; but that it is really an evil, meriting the strictures with which the teacher visits it, is more than they believe. What deceives them is this. They call to mind the events of a particular hour. There was during that hour, according to their recollection, a general attention to study, and no special disorder; perhaps some three or four of the pupils noted for talking. This talking, too, may have been about the lesson, or at all events was not such as to distract very perceptibly the current of instruction. Hence the inference that a moderate amount of talking, such as that was, is perfectly consistent with decorum and progress.

So it is. But what is to secure this moderate amount? What right have you to talk that is not enjoyed by your neighbor? If one may talk, so may all; if one does it, unchecked, so will all, as you very well know. How is the teacher to know whether you are talking about the lesson, or about the last cricket-match?

This is a perfectly plain question, and I press you to an answer. There is no practical medium between unlimited license to talk — against which you would yourself be the first to protest — and an entire prohibition. I put it to your conscience, whether you do not believe, were this rule strictly and in good faith observed, that the interests of the school, and your own interest, comfort, and honor, would be greatly promoted? Is the inconvenience which this rule imposes so great, or your habit of self-indulgence so strong, that you cannot, or will not, forego a slight temporary gratification for so substantial and lasting a benefit?

7. You will avoid much of the difficulty of observing this rule, if you give heed to the next counsel which I have now to give, and that is, that you economize carefully your time in school. On this point some excellent and conscientious pupils occasionally err. They are very faithful in home preparation; very attentive at lectures; very industrious in discharging any set duty. But they have not yet learned the true secret of all economy, whether of time, money, or any other good,— namely, the knowing how to use well the odds and ends. Take care of the pence, was Franklin's motto. If you once have the secret of occupying usefully, in studious preparation, or in wise repetition, all those little intervals of interrupted instruc-

tion, which necessarily occur throughout the day, you will in the first place almost insure for yourself an entire freedom from demerit marks of every kind; you will secondly add materially to your intellectual progress; and, lastly, you will acquire a habit of the utmost value in every station and walk in life; and, depend upon it, the habits you acquire at school, are of all your acquisitions by far the most important.

8. But I would be false to my most settled convictions, were I to stop here. I have been a teacher of the young nearly all my life, and as the result of such a life-long professional experience, I have no conviction more abiding than this, that *the fear of God is the beginning of knowledge.* I believe that mental growth is just as directly the gift of God as bodily growth; that the healthy action of the mind is as much dependent on his good pleasure as the healthy action of the bodily functions. God has not only made one mind superior to another, but of two minds naturally equal, he can, at his sovereign pleasure, make one grow and expand more rapidly than another. As he can give symmetry and strength to your limbs, and clothe your features with beauty and grace, so he can make you quick of apprehension, clear of discernment, ready and tenacious to remember, delicate in your appreciation of what is beautiful. While, therefore, you are diligent in your studies, remember that the reward of your labor, after all, is the gift of God. You will neglect one essential means of intellectual progress, if you neglect prayer. I mean, not prayer in general, but specific prayer for God's blessing on your studies; prayer that God will bless your

efforts to learn. Keep your mind, while engaged in study, in a habitual state of expectancy, especially when grappling with intellectual difficulties, as if inwardly looking up for help to that all-knowing Spirit, who alone, of all beings, acts directly on our spirits. I cannot doubt that one who studies in such a frame of mind, will advance in his intellectual progress more rapidly for it. I have a most assured conviction that prayer is a direct and important means of mental growth. Not only will the fear of God restrain you from many of the usual hindrances to study, of which I have already spoken, but a truly devout spirit is the very best state of mind for learning, even for learning purely intellectual truth.

There are other and higher motives, why you should cultivate, habitually, the fear of God. Of these motives, it is not my office to speak now. They are often pressed upon your attention. The one point to which I direct you now, is the importance of such a state of mind to your making the best, and surest, and noblest kind of mental growth. If you would grow rapidly in knowledge, grow symmetrically and beautifully, with all your faculties in harmonious preparation and dependence, fear God. Keep your spirit in habitual intercourse and communion with that Almighty Spirit who is the source of all knowledge and wisdom. In the school-room, at your desk, in your recitations, and your exercises of every kind, let the thought that the eye of a loving Father is upon you, diffuse habitually a calm and sweet peace through your spirit, and depend upon it, you will not find your mental vision dimmed by moving in so pure and serene an atmosphere. There are no quickeners to knowledge equal to love, reverence, and earnest prayer.

Let me, in conclusion, tender you my best wishes for your success in the career now before you. That success depends, in no small degree, upon the feeling and spirit with which you begin. Only summon up your mind to a serious and determined resolution at the outset; aim high; do not flinch at self-denial; rise above the unworthy suspicion that this or that teacher is unfair to you; resist the disposition to shirk those studies that you find disagreeable or difficult; keep clear of every kind and degree of trickery; come straight up to a full and strict compliance with every rule; lay your plans to occupy usefully each golden moment of leisure; cultivate a constant sense of dependence upon God for success in study: and your success will be as certain as is the wish for it, which I once more, most respectfully and affectionately, tender you.

---

3. *To a Young Lady on Leaving a Boarding-School.*

You are about to leave school. The occasion is one certainly that cannot fail to awaken reflection. I suppose that no young lady, who had been at a place of education as long as you have been here, ever left it without serious thought. The excitement of the examination, the busy whirl of preparation for leaving, even the exhilarating anticipations of home-going, cannot entirely shut out from your mind the sober truth that the end of school-days is only the beginning of another career,—a career, the issue of which you can neither foresee, nor can you be indifferent to it. Let us talk a little about this.

The day on which a young man ends his College course is called, by an apparent misnomer, "Commencement" day; that is, the day of commencing, or beginning. I understand very well that the name has a definite historical origin,—that in the old English Colleges, from which our American Colleges were modelled, the young man, on this day, begins his career as a Bachelor of Arts. His academical rank "commences" and dates from this point. But there would be a beautiful appropriateness in the term, even if it had no such special historical origin. The exit from the curriculum of the College or School, is, in truth, only the entrance into a more extended course. When your studies are nominally ended, they have really only begun. The longer you live, the more will you understand that the period of school-going is not the only, or even the main time of learning. The more thoroughly you have been taught here, the more certainly will you be a learner hereafter. I want no better test of the character of a school than the extent to which the idea prevails among its pupils and alumni, that it is a place for "finishing" one's studies. The idea is on a par with that of the young Miss who reported that she had read through Latin!

There is, it is true, in this School, a definite curriculum of studies, and that curriculum you have honorably completed. You have just been received by public acknowledgment into the community of educated women. But you will be false to the honorable sisterhood, false, I am sure, to all the teachings you have received here, if you entertain for a moment the thought that no further intellectual acquisitions are before you. The branches which you have learned thus far are chiefly valuable to you for the power they have given you to make still further improvement. The studies pursued at school, and during the period of youth, are mainly intended for promoting intellectual growth, for giving us power, for perfecting our mental machinery. Our real acquisitions come afterward. I speak, of course, of those who occupy the higher stations in society. To one who has to earn his bread by mere bodily toil, the few studies for which he has leisure in youth, must, of course, be such as are directly serviceable in his calling. But to those who claim to belong to the educated portion of the community, school studies are of right directed more to the development of the mental and moral powers, than to positive acquisition. Your instructors return you to your friends and your home with a mind enlarged, with a taste refined, with a judgment corrected, ready to take your place and act well your part, as an educated woman. But remember, she is not an educated woman, who knows no more this year than she did last. True education is growth, and it never stands still. The tree which has ceased to grow, has begun to decay.

This, then, is the one thought that I would have you take away with you from school. Give no place to the idea that henceforth books and study and elegant culture are to be laid aside. It would be a dishonor to your School, and a mistake of the first magnitude for yourself.

Perhaps you will appreciate this point more adequately, if you will turn your thoughts inward for a moment, and reflect upon the change which has been quietly going on in your own self and during your residence here. One whose occupation calls him almost daily to communicate his ideas to young persons, either by formal address, or by more familiar ways, feels to a greater degree, perhaps, than any other person can, the change to which I refer. I mean that increased quickness of intellectual apprehension produced by a judicious and symmetrical course of study. Let me give you an instance. It fell to my lot, not long since, to address a School containing three hundred young ladies, all boarders, all over seventeen years of age. They were the best audience I ever had. Among them was not one, who did not appear to be intelligent and thoughtful, and with a mind more or less disciplined. But there were perceptible differences among them, and it is to this point that I would direct your attention. They were divided into four distinct classes, having attended the School severally one, two, three, and four years, and they were arranged before me in the order of their seniority as classes. The discourse was long and didactic, and portions of it were not easy to follow, containing a discussion of a rather abstruse point in mental philosophy. Now it seemed to me, on concluding the address, that I could have gone through that assembly, and marked with tolerable accuracy, class by class, just where each class ended and another class began, simply by what I had read in the faces of my young auditors. It was written as plainly upon those upturned faces, as was the discourse itself upon the manuscript before me. Those who had been four years in the School, undoubtedly learned manifold more from the exercise than the junior classes did. I could see it in the delivery of every paragraph. Such is the uniform result of a proper course of study. It enables the student to grasp new truths with increased ease and readiness. We, who are teachers, feel this the moment we undertake to communicate our thoughts to an audience. The consequence is, we involuntarily measure what has been done educationally for a class of young persons, by the development which has been given to their powers,— by the manifest facility which they have gained for making further gains. That young woman is best educated who is best prepared to learn.

Let me, then, renew the appeal to your own consciousness. Think for a moment upon the change which has been wrought in your own self during your career here. Compare your present self with that other self that you may remember some three or four years back. How much more you can accomplish now than you could then! How much more clearly you can follow out a train of reasoning! How much more easily you can compass an argument! How much more you can enjoy what is beautiful! How much more quickly and accurately you can remember! How much more you can command your attention! Whence this change, and what does it purport? It means that you are educated. You have now a degree of mental power that you had not then. Your own consciousness tells you that you are now just in the condition to enter upon your harvest. The field is before you. You are girded for the work. And will you now indolently lay aside the sickle, and let the golden grain fall to the ground ungathered? Could there be a more egregious mistake? Last week, I saw from my window two parent birds tempting their young fledglings from the nest. Day by day, week by week, I had seen the child-birds growing and gaining strength. Their muscles were now well developed, their bodies were clothed with feathers, they had learned to use their wings,—they could fly. Would it not have been passing strange, had they continued as they were, contented to cower and to crawl, when they had acquired the power to soar? And will *you* be content to remain forever only a fledgling, satisfied with having acquired the power of rising, but never actually using the wings which these years of honorable industry have given you?

Some of your sex are willing to admit the force of this argument when applied to men. A man, after graduating, is expected of course to continue his studies. His whole profession is one continued study. But somehow, it is thought, this truth does not hold good for women. Let me hope that *you* at least will not harbor such a notion. Whatever may be said of "women's rights," one right certainly, and one duty, is to keep yourself abreast of the other sex in continued mental growth and culture, and in general intelligence. If you would awaken true respect in my sex, and I hold it a not unworthy ambition, you must in this matter do as we do, at least as those of us do who are worth your consideration at all. You must perseveringly, every year, add to your intellectual acquisitions. You must continue steadily to grow in knowledge and mental power. Do not cease your studies, because you have ceased going to school. Manage to have some elegant accomplishment or acquisition always in hand. A woman who is wise in this matter, never passes her prime. I speak not, of course, of the decrepitude of old age and of the decay of the faculties. But so long as the faculties remain unimpaired, a woman may become, and should aim to become, increasingly attractive, as she advances in years. Poets sing of sweet sixteen. Let me assure you, a woman may be charming at sixty. Mrs. Madison even at seventy was the most attractive woman in Washington.

In society, how soon one feels the difference between a person who reads, and one who does not read. Two ladies may be of the same age. They may dress alike. They may have the same advantages of person. They may move in the same social circle. Yet you will not have been ten minutes in their society, though the conversation has been on only the most common topics of the day, before you will feel that the one woman, though at thirty or forty, is still only a superannuated school-girl, with even less resources than when she left the seminary, while the other is a delightful companion for persons of any age, with ready knowledge for whatever turn the conversation may take, and so abounding in resources as not even to be open to the temptation of making a display of them. The one can talk only so long as the conversation turns on dress, gossip, or the discussion of private character. In listening to the talk of such a woman, you hardly hear a sentence which is not based upon personalities. Her mind has not been fed and nurtured from day to day with beautiful and noble thoughts, with history and science and general knowledge. She may be amiable. She may have personal beauty. But you find her empty and vapid, and you weary of her, in spite of the very best intentions of being interested. How different the woman who, in spite of social exactions, and even of accumulating domestic duties, and of the time-consuming tax of dress, still keeps her mind fresh and growing, by means of reading and culture,— who is ever adding to her stores of knowledge some new science, to her varied skill some new attainment, —who has ever in hand some new book. It is true, indeed, that some ladies are blessed with more leisure for this purpose than others. But I fear it is not a question of more and less. It is too much a question of some and *none*. I hold that every woman is entitled to have, and by proper determination she may have, *some* time for personal improvement. Remember, we have duties to ourselves, as well as to others, and we have no duty to ourselves more sacred than this,— to rescue from our time some portion for the purpose of making ourselves more worthy of regard.

To undertake to suggest what particular studies you should pursue, in this larger school to which you are now admitted, would lead me into a train of remark entirely too extended. One single practical suggestion may perhaps be pardoned. Do not willingly relinquish the acquisitions already made. They are to you the true foundations for future improvement. You have fairly entered upon several important fields in the domain of science. You are familiar with the elements of Natural Philosophy, Chemistry, Botany, Physiology, Mental Philosophy, Rhetoric, and with the foundations of Mathematical Science. My advice is that in coming years you give to each of these branches, and of whatever else you have studied here, a stated systematic review. You have some skill in drawing and painting. Let not so graceful an accomplishment die out from your fingers. You excel in music. I need not say, if you would retain this excellence, you must give time to practice and study. So, whatever talent or attainment you now have, let it be your fixed purpose not to let it pass from your possession. Keep what you have, whatever else you may fail to do. To this end, as I said before, give to each of your school studies an occasional well-considered review. You will then always have in your mind certain fixed points, to which the miscellaneous knowledge picked up in your general reading will adhere, and around which it will accumulate in organized form. New studies, too, will naturally affiliate with the old, and will be easy and pleasant just in proportion as you keep the knowledge that you now have, fresh and bright.

Besides this general advice, there is one accomplishment in particular, which I would earnestly recommend to you, as I am in the habit of doing to all of your sex. Cultivate assiduously the ability to read well. I stop to particularize this, because it is a thing so very much neglected, and because it is so very elegant, charming, and lady-like an accomplishment. Where one person is really interested by music, twenty are pleased with good reading. Where one person is capable of becoming a skilful musician, twenty may become good readers. Where there is one occasion suitable for the exercise of musical talent, there are twenty for that of reading. The culture of the voice necessary for reading well, gives a delightful charm to the same voice in conversation. Good reading is the natural exponent and vehicle of all good things. It is the most effective of all commentaries upon the works of genius. It seems to bring dead authors to life again, and makes us sit down familiarly with the great and good of all ages.

Did you ever notice what life and power the Holy Scriptures have, when well read? Have you ever heard of the wonderful effects produced by Elizabeth Fry among the hardened criminals of Newgate, by simply reading to them the parable of the Prodigal Son? Princes and peers of the realm, it is said, counted it a privilege to stand in those dismal corridors, among felons and murderers, merely to share with them the privilege of witnessing the marvellous pathos which genius, taste, and culture could infuse into that simple story.

What a fascination there is in really good reading! What a power it gives one! In the hospital, in the chamber of the invalid, in the nursery, in the domestic and the social circle, among chosen friends and companions, how it enables you to minister to the amusement, the comfort, the pleasure of dear ones, as no other art or accomplishment can. No instrument of man's devising can reach the heart, as does that most wonderful instrument, the human voice. It is God's special gift and endowment to his chosen creatures. Fold it not away in a napkin. If you would double the value of all your other acquisitions;

if you would add immeasurably to your own enjoyment, and to your power of promoting the enjoyment of others, cultivate with incessant care this Divine gift. No music below the skies is equal to that of pure, silvery speech from the lips of a man or woman of high culture.

---

4. *To a Pupil on Entering a Normal School.*

You have entered upon a new and untried path. As one having been often over this way, and well acquainted with the features of the country before you, its lights and shadows, its roses and its thorns, its safe walks and its hidden pitfalls, I desire to talk with you a while before you enter upon the untried scene.

1. First of all let me say to you, we give you a most hearty welcome. We are glad to see you here, and we tender to you in advance a warm and ready sympathy in the many little worries, annoyances, and discouragements that surely await you. For myself I may truly say, that, outside of my own home, I have no greater happiness than to be among my pupils, and few things could pain me more than to believe that any one who had been for any considerable time my pupil would not almost unconsciously claim me as a friend; and it is an unceasing well-spring of joy for me to know that among your companions are many who, in time of trouble or difficulty or anxiety of any kind, would come to the Principal of the School, as sure of sympathy as if going to their own mother.

This freedom of intercourse between teachers and their

pupils, this mutual exchange of confidence on one side and of sympathy on the other, is a source of good and a source of pleasure, which neither you nor we, my young friend, can afford to forego; and if in the expression of this thought I have indulged in a rather unseemly use of the first person singular, it is not because I would claim for myself anything peculiar in this matter, but because, from my years and my position, I can perhaps, better than my associates, afford to speak out thus the inward promptings of the heart. We *all* give you the right hand of fellowship, and trust it will not be many weeks, or days even, before you shall feel that you have here a home as well as a school, friends as well as teachers.

2. A very common feeling at the beginning of a course of study, is a feeling of discouragement. Nearly all the studies are new, and you enter upon each with fresh eagerness. Now, it is in the nature of every study while it is new, to seem boundless. Under the guiding hand of a skilful teacher, its limits and capabilities are stretched out in one direction and another, interminable vistas spread out in the distance, and portentous difficulties rise up before the imagination, until the mind is bewildered.

There is not one, of the formidable lists of studies before you, that might not of itself, so great are its capabilities, occupy your whole time. When you find yourself called to grapple at once with four or five such studies, to measure yourself with competitors, many of whom have had opportunities of preparation greatly superior to your own, and in the presence of teachers to whom the whole subject is as familiar and as plain as the alphabet, and when, in addition, the methods of recitation are for the most part new and strange, you are very apt to become discouraged, to feel that you shall never learn to recite in the manner required, that you can never master the difficulties before you. This feeling arises most frequently in the best class of minds, those most conscientious in regard to duty and most capable of comprehending the full length and breadth and depth of a subject. The shallow and the trifling are never troubled with the kind of difficulties now under consideration.

I address myself to you, my young friend, because I know you have come here with an earnest purpose, with a mind acute enough to see something of the vast work before you, and I say to you, as one who has had large experience in conducting other pilgrims over the same track, never lose heart. Difficulties which now seem insurmountable, will gradually disappear; subjects which now seem impenetrable, will soon lighten up. Did you never enter a room in the dark? At first the apartment is a universal blank. After a while, as your eyes become adjusted to the place, one article after another of the furniture becomes outlined to the vision, until at length, especially if approaching day lends some additional rays of light, the whole scene stands out perfectly defined. So it is in entering upon a new study. Many a passage in it will seem to you at first a worse than Serbonian bog — a cave of impenetrable and undistinguishable darkness. But draw not back. Look steadily on. Light will come in time. Your power of seeing will, with every new trial, receive adjustment and growth, and you will in the end see with full and open vision where now you have only dim glimpses and guesses. Do not be discouraged, therefore, if at first you fail, or seem to yourself to fail, in almost every recitation you undertake. What seems impossible to-day, will be only next to impossible to-morrow, and only very difficult the day after. Your failures are often only the proofs that you have a glimpse at least of something below the surface of things. A discouraged pupil is never a source of anxiety to me. It is only the self-confident and over-wearing that are hopeless.

3. I have spoken of recitations. Let me urge you to form some definite idea of what a recitation is, and what kind of a recitation you, as a pupil of a Normal School, should aim to make. And first of all, on this point, let me say, the mere answering of questions, and especially, the mere response of yes and no to questions, is not reciting,—assuredly not such reciting as is to fit you for the office of a teacher. And, in the next place, let me say, that repeating verbatim the words of the book, is not the method of recitation at which you should aim. I do not agree with those who would dissuade you entirely from cultivating the faculty and enriching the stores of memory. Not only memory, in its general exercise, but a purely verbal memory, is important. In your lessons, are many things, rules, definitions, and so forth, that should be learned with the most literal exactness, and should be so fixed in the memory that they will come at your bidding, in any place, at any moment. There are, too, in some of your books, passages from noble authors, which furnish food and nourishment to the soul, and which the mind

craves in the very form and lineaments of their birth — passages which are like nuggets of virgin gold, or coins from the mint of some great sovereign in the realms of thought. They form a part of your wealth, and you want them, neither clipped, nor defaced, nor alloyed, but with every word and point exactly as it came from the hand of the master. These precious gems of thought, the garnered wealth of the ages, will not be neglected by any one who is wise. Treasure up in your intellectual storehouse as many of them as you can possibly compass, only with this proviso, be careful to select for this purpose the very best out of the great abundance that is before you, and make thorough work in what you do attempt to commit to memory. The act of memorizing will at once strengthen the faculty of memory itself, and will enrich you otherwise. By all means, therefore, learn by heart the leading definitions and rules of your text-books, and choice passages from all famous authors. But do not attempt in this way to commit to memory, or to recite verbatim, the pages of your history, geography, rhetoric, and so forth. Such a practice would be a most unwise waste of your time, and would cause a weakening, rather than a strengthening, of your faculties.

Let me tell you exactly what I mean by reciting. Your teacher goes to the board and, chalk in hand, explains to the class some point which they seem not to have apprehended. That is my idea of reciting. First get thorough possession of the thoughts or facts of the lesson, and then, imagining the class and the teacher to be ignorant of the subject, explain it to them, just as you will expect to do when the time comes that you will have a class of your own to instruct. It will aid you in preparing thus to recite a lesson, if in your rooms you will go over it aloud to each other, you and your room-mate, taking alternate portions. Such a method of preparation will doubtless require some time. But one lesson so prepared will be worth more to you than a whole week of study conducted in the ordinary manner. Remember, that in a Normal School your object is, not merely to get knowledge, but to learn how to communicate what you have learned. First then go over a topic till you are sure you understand it. Then go over it again and again until you can recite readily and perfectly every part of it, in its order. Then practise yourself in telling it in your own words, aloud, if possible, to somebody else, until you can make the narration or explanation continuously, from beginning to end, and without the possibility of being thrown out or confused by any amount of interruptions. Then at length are you prepared to recite.

Is this standard of recitation too high? Is it not what every one of your teachers does daily, and what you yourself will have to do the very first time you take your position as a teacher of others?

4. This leads me by a natural transition to the subject of *study*. You need to learn how to study, as much as you need to learn how to recite. Endeavor then to get some definite idea in your mind of what it is really to study. Mere reading is not study. Muttering the words over in a low, gurgling tone, or letting them glide in a soft, half-audible ripple upon your lips, is not study.

Going over the lesson in a listless, dreamy way, one eye on the book and one eye ready for whatever is going on in other parts of the room, is not study. Study is work. Study is agony. The whole soul must be roused, its every energy put forth, with a fixed, rapt attention, like that of a man struggling with a giant. Study, worthy of the name, forgets for the time every thing else, excludes every thing else, is incapable of being diverted by any thing else, the whole internal and external man being bent upon making just one thing its own. Such study of course soon exhausts the energies. It cannot be long protracted, nor need it be protracted. Take rest in the season of rest; but, when you study, study with all your might. Throw your whole soul into it. One hour of such study accomplishes more than whole days of listless poring over books. And, remember, you cannot study in this manner by merely willing to do it. It is an art, requiring training and practice, and thorough mental discipline. You might as well, on seeing the Writing-Master executing those marvels of penmanship, or the Drawing-Teacher with deft fingers limning with ease forms of grace and beauty, resolve to go forthwith to the board and do the same thing, as expect, by a mere *sic volo*, to become a student. You are here to learn how to study, and the art will come to you only by slow progress, and after many trials.

Give up the illusion that absolute seclusion and silence are necessary to study. I do not say that they are not at times desirable. But they do not of themselves generate earnest thought. The vacant mind, that has not yet learned to think, is when thus left to solitude and stillness, quite as likely to go a wool-gathering, or to fall asleep, as to wrestle with some hard uninviting train of thought. The appliances and the invitations to mental application, if we have really learned to study, must be mainly in ourselves, not in our surroundings. Besides, the greater part of the actual thinking and study, that has to be done by those in professional life, that will have to be done by you, when you enter upon the practice of your profession as a teacher, must be done in circumstances not of your own choosing, just as time and opportunity may offer, by snatches, and at odd intervals, and often in the midst of distracting sights and sounds. I venture to say that three fourths of the graduates of this school, who are now teaching, have no opportunity for daily study and preparation for the duties of the school-room, except that afforded by a seat in the evening in the common sitting-room of the family, surrounded by children that are not always models of behavior, and within sight and hearing of all the petty details of household life. It is not therefore in itself undesirable that a part at least of your study at school should be performed in a common room, where there are some temptations to be resisted, some distractions to be ignored. Acquiring the ability to study without distraction in the presence of others and in the midst even of confusion and noise, is as important to you as is the learning how to think aloud, in the presence of a class, which I have defined to be the true nature of a recitation. The ability to study and the ability to recite are intimately correlated, and the symptoms of both are unmistakable to the practised eye and ear. I know just as well, by a glance of the eye on entering a study-room, what pupils are making intellectual growth, as I do on entering the class-room and listening to the recitations. One might as well feign to be in a fever, as to feign study. Nothing but the thing itself can assume its appearance.

5. I approach my next subject of remark with some hesitation. Yet on no point, in the whole theory of mental action, have I a more fixed and assured conviction. Perhaps I may explain my meaning better, if I introduce it with one or two comparisons.

Action of every kind, mental or material, is to be aided or accelerated, if at all, by forces of the same kind with the primary force. If a certain amount of weight avoirdupois will not make the scale kick the beam, we may produce the effect by laying on the requisite number of additional pounds,—by adding force of the same kind with the original. If the flame of one candle does not produce the illumination required for a particular effort, the addition of a second or a third will. If we wish to increase the speed of a locomotive, we do not whistle to it, or whip it, or say "get up;" we add steam. If on the other hand we wish our horse to travel faster, we use a motive addressed to his nature. We appeal to his generosity, his pride, or his fear. So mental action is influenced and induced by forces of the same nature with itself. One mind influences powerfully another mind, working upon us often, too, by mysterious influences that elude analysis. The influence of mind upon mind, other things being equal, is in proportion to the degree of perfection in which these three conditions exist, to wit, the fulness of accord and sympathy between the minds that are brought into contact, the closeness of the contact, and the greatness and power of the influencing and controlling mind. These three points hardly need explanation or argument. Nothing is more obvious than that a mind fully in sympathy with another, does by that very circumstance exercise an increased mental power on that other. In like manner we all feel daily how our minds are lifted up, enlarged, enlightened, strengthened, by intercourse with one of powerful intellect. And how often have we felt, when ourselves wishing to influence any one, particularly when wishing to influence one much younger and weaker than ourselves, that we might accomplish our ends the better, if we could only know certainly and exactly what he was thinking, if we could as it were actually get into the chamber of his soul. This indeed we can never do. We think sometimes that we come very near to each other. But after all we never touch. Between my mind and yours, between yours and that of the most intimate friend you have in the world, there is a barrier, high as heaven, deep as hell, impenetrable as adamant. Thus far can we come and no farther. We can never enter into the soul of any human being. No human being can ever enter into ours. Yet, my dear pupil, did it never occur to you, that there is One Mind, and that a mind of infinitely great and transcendent power, to which there is no such barrier, and that this transcendent, all-knowing, all-powerful mind, is continually in direct contact with the very essence of your mind? Can I influence your thinking faculties, and cannot the infinite God, who made those faculties? Can He who gave our bodies all their power of growth and strength, not give growth and strength to our minds? I do not profess to understand how the divine mind acts upon the human mind. I cannot always understand even how one human mind acts upon another. But of the fact I make no more question, than I do of the powers of flame, of steam, or of gravitation. And, as one set here to guide you in your mental progress, in all sober earnestness, I exhort you devoutly to invoke the aid of the Holy Ghost in the promotion of your studies — not merely to help you to use your acquisitions rightly, for his honor and the good of your kind, but to help you in making those acquisitions. If you would rise superior to discouragement, if you would acquire that mental discipline which is to enable you to study, and to recite and to teach in the very best and highest manner, pray. Call mightily upon God the Holy Ghost, who is after all the great educator and teacher of the human race. Carry your feeble lamp to the great fountain of light and radiance. Put your heart into full accord and sympathy with that of your dear elder Brother. Wrestle mightily with God in secret, as one that feels the burden of a great want. Thus, my dear pupil, will you best fit yourself for the duties of a student and of a teacher. For, believe me, there is sound philosophy as well as religion, in the utterance of the wise man, "The fear of the Lord is the beginning of knowledge." Surely that man is a fool, who in cultivating mind, whether his own or that of another, neglects to invoke the aid of the Infinite Mind.

XXIX.

AN ARGUMENT FOR COMMON SCHOOLS.

THE argument for popular education is familiar and trite, and yet it needs to be occasionally re-stated and enforced. There is no community in which there is not a considerable number of persons grossly and dangerously ignorant, and there are many communities in which the majority of the people are in this condition. There is no community in which the importance of general education is over-estimated; there are unfortunately many communities in which education is held to be the least important of public interests. A brief discussion of the subject, therefore, can never be entirely out of place.

Before proceeding to the direct argument, let me notice some of the most common objections.

It is a not uncommon opinion, that the business of education should be left, like other kinds of business, to the laws of trade. It is said, if a carpenter is wanted in any community, or a blacksmith, or a tailor, or a lawyer, or a doctor, carpenters, blacksmiths, tailors, lawyers, and doctors will make their appearance. If a store is wanted, a store will spring up. Why not a school-house? Those who use this argument forget the essential difference between the two classes of wants to be supplied. All men equally feel the distress, if naked, or hungry, or sick, or suffering from any material want. The poor man, no less than the rich, feels the pinchings of hunger, and will exert himself to remedy the evil. The sick man, even more than the well, appreciates the value of medicine and the necessity of a physician. Not so in the matter of knowledge. A man must himself be educated, to understand the value of education. There are exceptions, of course. Yet it is substantially true, that the want of education is not one of those felt and pinching necessities that compel men's attention, and that consequently may be left to shift for themselves. A man who has himself enjoyed the blessing of a good education, expects to provide schools for his children, as much as he expects to provide for them food and clothing. The wants of their minds are to him pressing realities, as much as are the wants of their bodies. Not so with the ignorant and debased neighbors, who live within stone's throw of his dwelling. They, from their own experience, know nothing better, and are quite content, both for themselves and their children, to live on in the debased condition in which we see them. If these wretched creatures are ever moved to seek a higher style of living and being, the movement must originate outside of themselves. It is a case in which the man of higher advantages must think and act for those below him. It is a case in which people have a pressing need without knowing it, and in which consequently the laws of supply and demand do not meet the emergency.

Another common opinion on this subject is that private enterprise is adequate to meet the want. Private enterprise in education is not indeed to be discarded. Where the community as a whole, in its organized capacity, will do nothing, let individuals do what they can. In such cases, let those who appreciate the advantages of education, concert measures for the establishment of schools and the employment of teachers, and for inducing parents who are indifferent to send their children. By these private efforts, the community may be gradually awakened to the importance of the subject, and so be induced to take it up on their own account. But private benevolence is not sufficient for so great a work. Private benevolence besides is apt to be fitful. It is at best subject to interruption by death and by reverses of fortune, while the cause is one which especially demands steadiness and continuity. The means for educating a community or a city should no more be subject to interruption, than the means of lighting it, or of supplying it with water.

The argument for depending upon private enterprise for devising and providing the means for popular education, would apply equally well to matters of police, and to the protection of property. The strong-armed and the sagacious can take care of themselves. The stout-hearted and the good, by due concert and combination, could keep criminals in some check, even in a country where there were no courts of justice, or prisons, or detective police. But this is not the ordinary or the best mode of accomplishing the end, nor could it in any case be thoroughly efficient. The restraint and punishment of crime belong to society as a whole, in its sovereign capacity. To the same society belongs the duty of seeing that its members do not fall into degrading ignorance and vice. God, in ordaining human society, had something higher in view than merely providing for the punishment of crime. Our Heavenly Father would have his children raised to the full enjoyment of their privileges as social and rational beings, and he seems to have established society for this very end, among others, that there may be an agency and a machinery adequate and fitted to drag even the unwilling out of the mire into which they have fallen. Without such an interposition on the part of society as a whole, the work will not be done. The mass of the people will remain in ignorance in every community, in which the community as such does not provide the means of education and general enlightenment.

It is often urged against common schools, that they tend to impair parental obligation. Let us look this objection fairly in the face. The argument is stated as follows. If the community, in its organic capacity as a civil government, provides systematically for the instruction of the young, the system, just so far as it is successful and complete, does away with the necessity for any other provision. The parent, finding this work done to his hands, feels no necessity of looking after it himself, and so gradually loses all sense of obligation on the subject. Such a result, it is contended, is in contravention of the plainest dictates of nature and the most positive teachings of religion, both nature and religion requiring it as a primary duty of every parent to give his child a suitable education.

In meeting this objection, the friends of common schools agree with the objector to the fullest extent in asserting the imperative, universal, irrepealable duty of the parent to educate his own child. The duty is not the less binding on the parent, because a like duty, covering the same point, rests also on the community. The interests involved are so momentous, that God in his wise ordination has given them a double security. It is a case in which two distinct parties are both separately required to see one and the same thing done. It is like taking two indorsers to a note. The obligation of one indorser is not impaired, because another man equally with himself is bound for payment. If a child grows up in ignorance and vice, while God will undoubtedly hold the parent responsible, he will also not hold the community guiltless. Both parties will be guilty before him, both parties will be punished. A man is bound to maintain a certain amount of cleanliness about his habitation. If he fails to do so, and if in consequence of this failure the atmosphere around him becomes tainted and malarious, he and his will suffer. Disease and death will visit his abode. But the consequences will not end here. The infection will extend. The whole community will be affected by it. The whole community, equally with the individual, are bound to see that the cause of the infection is removed. The infection will not spare the community because the individual has generated it, nor will it spare the individual because the community has failed to remove it. Each party has a duty and a peril of its own in regard to the same matter.

The fact is, individuals and the community are so bound together, that on many points their obligations lie in coincident lines. The matter of education is one of these points. God has ordained the parental relation, and has implanted the parental affections, for this very reason, among others, that the faculties of the helpless young immortal may have due training and development,—that this development may not be left to chance, like that of a worthless weed, but may have the protection and guardianship which are the necessary birthright of every rational creature brought into being by the voluntary act of another. But God has ordained society also for this same end, among others, namely, that his rational creatures may have a competent agency, bound by the laws and necessities of its own welfare to make adequate provision for the instruction and education of every human being. The one duty does not conflict with the other. The one obligation does not impair the other. Both lie in coincident lines.

But, as a question of fact, is it true that common schools impair the sense of obligation in the minds of parents in regard to the duty of educating their children? I affirm the fact to be exactly the contrary. Those communities in which there are no common schools, and in which the people generally are in a state of deplorable ignorance, are precisely those in which the sense of parental obligation on this point is at the lowest ebb. Go to a region of country in which not one man in ten can read and write, and you will find that not one man in ten will care whether his children are taught to read and write. Those communities on the contrary which have the best and most complete system of common schools, and in which this system has prevailed longest and has taken most complete hold of the public mind, are the very ones in which individuals will be found most keenly alive to the importance of the subject, and in which a parent will be regarded as a monster, if his children are allowed to grow up uneducated.

The objection, therefore, has no foundation either in fact or in reason. There is moreover another consideration not to be overlooked. In this matter of education, it is after all but a small part which the school does for a child. The main part of the child's education always takes place at home. The teacher is at best only an aid to the parent, supplementing the influences of the home and the street. The child is taking lessons continually from the father and mother, whether they mean it or not. Every teacher knows how much more rapidly a child improves at school, whose parents are well educated, and how difficult it is to teach a child who at home lives in an atmosphere of profound ignorance. The mind of the one whose home is a region of darkness and intellectual torpor, will be dwarfed and distorted, no matter what the efforts of its teachers. The mind of the one, on the contrary, whose home is the abode of intellectual light, warmth, and sunshine, will have a corresponding growth and expansion at school. There is a continual unconscious tuition, good or bad, received from the very atmosphere of the family. Besides this, there is a great deal of direct, active duty to be performed by the parent in the education of the child. No matter how good the school, or how faithful the teacher, there always remains much to be done by the parent, even in regard to the school duties. The parent must see that lessons are prepared, that the child is properly provided with books, that the meal times and the other arrangements of the household are such as to help forward the child's studies. There are a hundred things which the father and mother can do to help or to hinder the work of the school. A child, whose parents give proper home supervision over his studies, will, other things being equal, make twice the progress of one whose parents give the matter no attention. The community, therefore, in establishing common schools, does by no means take the whole matter of education out of the hands of the parent. On the contrary, it still leaves with him the most important and necessary of the duties connected with the education of his children, while it gives him aids for the performance of the remaining duties, which no private means can ordinarily supply.

I come, however, to a much graver objection. It is urged against common schools, as organized in this country, that religious instruction is excluded from them, and that without this element they only tend to make educated villains. Education, it is said, without the restraining and sanctifying influences of religion, only puts into the hands of the multitude greater power for evil. If this objection is valid, the most enlightened and Christian communities of the world have made, and are making, an enormous mistake. Yet the objection is urged with seriousness by men whose purity of motive is above question, and whose personal character gives great weight to their opinions. The objection originated in England, where all attempts to make legislative provision for the education of the common people have been steadily resisted by a potential party in the established church. The arguments put forth in the English religious journals have been reproduced in the journals here, and have in many instances awakened the apprehensions of serious-minded persons. It is worth while, therefore, to give the subject some distinct consideration.

In the first place, the facts are not exactly as stated by those making the objection. Though little direct religious instruction may be given in the common school, there is usually a large amount of religious influence. A great majority of the teachers of our common schools are professing Christians. Very many of them are among our most active Sabbath-school teachers. Now a truly godly man or woman, at the head of a school, though never speaking a word directly on the subject of religion, yet by the power of a silent, consistent example, exerts a continual Christian influence. In the second place, as a matter of fact, direct religious teaching is not entirely excluded from our public schools. I think, it by no means holds that prominent position in the course of study which it should hold. But it is not entirely excluded. The Bible, with very rare exceptions, is read daily in all our common schools. It is appealed to as ultimate authority in questions of history and morals. It is quoted for illustration in questions of taste. It is in many schools a text-book for direct study. In the third place, nine out of ten of the children of the week-day school attend the Sabbath-school. The Sabbath-school supplements the instructions of the week-day school. The case, therefore, is not that of an education purely intellectual. Moral and religious instruction accompanies the instruction in worldly knowledge. The Sabbath-school, the church, and the family, by their combined and ceaseless activities, infuse into our course of elementary education a much larger religious ingredient than a stranger might suppose, who should confine his examination to a mere inspection of our common schools, or to the reading of the annual reports of our educational boards.

But apart from all these considerations, taking the question in its naked form, is it true that mere intellectual education has the tendency alleged? I do not believe it. The constitution of the human mind gives no warrant for such an inference. Recorded, indisputable facts, overwhelmingly disprove it. So far is it from being true that the mere diffusion of knowledge has a tendency to make men knaves and infidels, I believe the very opposite to be true. Knowledge is the natural ally of religion. To hold otherwise, is to disparage and dishonor religion — to imply, if not to say, that ignorance is the mother of devotion.

There is an inborn antagonism between the intellectual and the sensual nature of man. If you give to the intellect no development, you leave the senses as the ruling power. We see this strikingly illustrated in the idiotic, who are for the most part disgustingly sensual. Among a population grossly ignorant and uneducated, sensualism prevails in its most appalling forms. The man is a sensualist, simply because he knows no higher pleasures. He is degraded, because he has no motives to be otherwise. He is barely above a brute. The amount of crime, of the coarsest and most debasing character, among the uneducated peasantry of England, is almost incredible. Here is a description of an English peasant of the present day, given by a competent unimpeached witness, himself an Englishman. I quote from a work on "The Social Condition and Education of the People of England," by Joseph Kay, Esq., of Trinity College, Cambridge, who was commissioned by the Senate of the University to travel for the purpose of examining into the social condition of the poorer classes. Says Mr. Kay: "You cannot address an English peasant, without being struck with the intellectual darkness which surrounds him. There is neither speculation in his eye nor intelligence in his countenance. His whole expression is more that of an animal than of a man. He is wanting too in the erect and independent bearing of a man. As a class, our peasants have no amusements beyond the indulgence of sense. In nine cases out of ten, recreation is associated in their minds with nothing higher than sensuality. About one half of our poor can neither read nor write, have never been in any school, and know little, or positively nothing, of the doctrines of the Christian religion, of moral duties, or of any higher pleasures than beer-drinking and spirit-drinking, and the grossest sensual indulgence. They live precisely like brutes, to gratify, so far as their means allow, the appetites of their uncultivated bodies, and then die, to go they have never thought, cared, or wondered whither. Brought up in the darkness of barbarism, they have no idea that it is possible for them to attain any higher condition; they are not even sentient enough to desire, with any strength of feeling, to change their situation; they are not intelligent enough to be perseveringly discontented; they are not sensible to what we call the voice of conscience; they do not understand the necessity of avoiding crime, beyond the mere fear of the police and the jail; they have unclear, indefinite, and undefinable ideas of all around them; they eat, drink, breed, work, and die; and while they pass through their brute-like existence here, the richer and more intelligent classes are obliged to guard them with police and standing armies, and to cover the land with prisons, cages, and all kinds of receptacles for the perpetrators of crime."

Surely it must be some hallucination of mind, which leads men to suppose that the diffusion of knowledge among such a population, even though it be only scientific and intellectual knowledge, can have any natural or general tendency adverse to religion and morals. Apart, however, from speculation, and as a pure question of fact, the recorded statistics of crime point unmistakably the other way. Criminal records the world over prove, beyond reasonable doubt, that the overwhelming majority of crimes are committed by persons deplorably ignorant. Intellectual education, therefore, I contend, even when deprived of its natural ally and adjunct, religious training, has no natural tendency to produce knaves and villains. On the contrary, it is a most efficient corrective and restraint of the evil and debasing tendencies of human nature. If the intellect is not so high a region in man's constitution as the moral powers, which I readily grant, it is at least above the mere sensual part, in which vice and crime have their chief spring and aliment. The question fortunately is one susceptible of a direct appeal to facts. Who are the men and women that people our jails and prisons? Are they persons of education, or are they in the main persons deplorably ignorant? What is the record of criminal statistics on this point?

I will quote a few of these statistics, from a great mass of similar evidence lying before me.

Out of 252,544 persons committed for crime in England and Wales, during a series of years, 229,300, or more than 90 per cent., are reported as uneducated, either entirely unable to read and write, or able to do so only very imperfectly; 22,159 could read and write, but not fluently; and only 1085 (*less than one half per cent. of the whole*) were what we call educated persons.

In nine consecutive years, beginning with the year 1837, only 28 educated females were brought to the bar of criminal justice in England and Wales, out of 7,673,633 females then living in that part of the United Kingdom; and in the year 1841, out of the same population, not one educated female was committed for trial.

In a special commission, held in 1842, to try those who had been guilty of rioting and disturbance in the manufacturing districts, out of 567 thus tried, 154 could neither read nor write, 155 could read only, 184 could read and write imperfectly, 73 could read and write well, and only one had received superior instruction.

In 1840, in 20 counties of England and Wales, with a population of 8,724,338, there were convicted of crime only 59 educated persons, or one for every 147,870 inhabitants. In 32 other counties, with a population of 7,182,491, the records furnished *not one convict* who had received more than the merest elements of instruction.

In 1841, in 15 English counties, with a population of 9,569,064, there were convicted only 74 instructed persons, or one to every 129,311 inhabitants, while the 25 remaining counties and the whole of Wales, with a population of 6,342,661, did not furnish one single conviction of a person who had received more than the mere elements of education.

In 1845, out of a total of 59,123 persons taken into custody, 15,263 could neither read nor write, and 39,659 could barely read, and could write very imperfectly.

In the four best taught counties of England, the number of schools being one for every seven hundred inhabitants, the number of criminal convictions was one a year for every 1108 inhabitants. In the four worst taught counties, the number of schools being one for every 1501 inhabitants, the number of convictions was one a year for every 550 inhabitants. That is, in one set of counties, the people were about twice as well educated as in the other, and one half as much addicted to crime. In other words, in proportion as the people were educated, were they free from crime.

Thrift and good morals usually keep pace with the spread of intelligence among the people. This has been the result in all those countries of Europe where good common schools are maintained, as in Iceland, Norway, Sweden, Denmark, Holland, Belgium, and most of the German States. Pauperism, with its attendant evils and crimes, is almost unknown in those countries, while in England, where the common people are worse educated than those of any Protestant nation in the world, pauperism has become an evil which her wisest statesmen have given up as unmanageable. In 1848, in addition to hundreds of persons assisted by charitable individuals, no less than 1,876,541 paupers (*one out of every eight of the population!*) were relieved by the boards of guardians of the poor, at an expense from the public purse of nearly thirty millions of dollars.

In our own country, the same pains have not been taken to collect statistics on this subject, because comparatively little controversy about it has existed here to call forth inquiry. We as a people have generally taken it for granted that popular education lessens crime and pauperism. Still, facts enough have been recorded to show the same results here as elsewhere. When an educated villain is convicted, like Monroe Edwards or Professor Webster, the fact becomes so notorious by means of the press, that it is unconsciously multiplied in our imagination, and we think the instances more numerous than they really are. We never think of the scores of obscure villains that are convicted every week all the year round. A quotation or two from the facts which have been recorded, will be sufficient to satisfy us on this point.

In the Ohio penitentiary, out of 276 inmates, nearly all were reported as ignorant, and 175 as grossly so.

In the Auburn prison, New York, out of 244 inmates, only 39 could read and write.

In the Sing Sing prison, no official record has been made

on this point. But the Rev. Mr. Luckey, for more than twenty years chaplain of the prison, is obliged by the prison regulations to superintend and read all the letters between the prisoners and their friends. In this manner he becomes personally acquainted with the condition of the convicts in regard to education. He reported a few months since to the writer of these pages, that while there are always some among the convicts who have been educated, yet the great mass of them are stolidly ignorant. There are usually between one and two hundred learning to read, and this does not include the half of those who are unable to read, as the attendance upon the class is voluntary, the accommodations are meagre, and most of the prisoners are indifferent to their own improvement. Not five in a hundred can write otherwise than in the most clumsy and awkward manner, and with the grossest blunders in orthography, and not more than two in a hundred can write a sentence grammatically. Out of the 700 then in prison, only three were liberally educated, and two of these were foreigners.

Throughout the State of New York, in 1841, the ratio of uneducated criminals to the whole number of uneducated persons was twenty-eight times as great as the ratio of educated inhabitants.

In view of the facts which have been given, and which might be multiplied to almost any extent, it is not easy to avoid the conclusion that mere intellectual education has some power to restrain men from the commission of crime. Assuredly, ignorance and sin are natural adjuncts and allies.

Schools undoubtedly cost something. The community

that undertakes to educate the masses, or the individual that undertakes to educate his children, must expect to have a serious bill to pay. It is a pernicious folly to inculcate the contrary. The advocate of popular education, who tries to persuade people into the experiment, under the assurance that the expense will be trifling, misleads his readers, and puts back the cause which he would fain put forward. But there is a most significant *per contra* in the account, and on this there is no danger of dwelling too much. Nothing is so costly as crime, and no preventive of crime is more efficient than education. Schoolhouses are cheaper than jails, teachers and books are a better security than handcuffs and policemen. There are educated villains, it is true. But they are rare, and they attract the greater attention by the very fact of their rarity. But go into a prison, or a criminal court, or a police court, and see who they are that mainly occupy the proceedings of our expensive machinery of criminal justice. Nine-tenths of those miserable creatures are in a state of most deplorable ignorance. Degraded, sensual, with no knowledge of anything better than the indulgence of the lowest passions, without mental resources, or any avenue to intellectual enjoyment, they often resort to crime from sheer want of something better to do. When Dr. Johnson was asked, "Who is the most miserable man?" his reply was, "The man who cannot read on a rainy day." There is profound meaning in the answer. The man who has been educated, who not only can read, but has acquired a taste for reading, and for reading of a proper kind, is rarely driven into low and debasing crime.

He has resources within himself, which are a counterpoise to the incitements of his animal nature. His awakened intellect and conscience also make him understand more clearly the danger and guilt of a life of crime. Many of the deeds which swell the records of our criminal courts spring from poverty, as every criminal lawyer well knows, and there is no remedy against extreme poverty so sure as education. The old adage says that knowledge is power. It is also wealth. A man with even an ordinary, common school education, can turn himself in a hundred ways, where a mere ignorant boor would be utterly helpless. The faculties are developed, ingenuity is quickened, the man's resources are enlarged. An educated man may be tempted to crime, but he is not driven into it, as hundreds are daily, by mere poverty, or by an intolerable hunger of the mind for enjoyment of some kind.

Schools, then, especially schools in which moral and religious truth is inculcated, are the most powerful means of lessening crime, and of lessening the costly and frightful apparatus of criminal administration. As schoolhouses and churches increase in the land, jails and prisons diminish. As knowledge is diffused, property becomes secure, and rises in value. A community, therefore, is bound to see that its members are properly educated, if for no other reason, in mere self-defence. The many must be educated, in order that the many may be protected. A great city is just as sacredly bound to provide for its teeming population the light of knowledge, as it is to provide material light for its streets. The one kind of illumination, equally with the other, is an essential part of its police.

No matter what the cost, the dark holes and alleys must be flooded with the light of truth, before which the owls and bats and vampyres of society will be scattered to the winds. A great city without schools would be a hell, — a seething caldron of vice, impurity, and crime. No man of sound mind would choose such a place for the residence of himself and family, who had the means of living in any other place. If we could suppose two cities entirely equal in other respects, but in one of them a superior and costly system of free schools, while the other spent not a dollar upon schools, but depended solely upon the rigors of the law and the strong arm of avenging justice for restraining the ignorant and corrupt masses, can there be any doubt which city would be the safest and most desirable place of residence?

Whatever view of this subject may be taken in other countries, we in this country are shut up to the necessity of popular education. We at least have no choice. Universal suffrage necessitates universal education. If we do not educate our people, educate universally, educate wisely and liberally, we can hardly expect to maintain permanently our popular institutions. The man's vote, who cannot read the names on the ballot which he throws into the box, counts just as much in deciding public affairs as yours, who are versed in statesmanship and political economy. He is a partner in the political firm. You can neither withdraw from the firm yourself, nor can you throw him out. In the absence of general education, this tremendous power of suffrage is something frightful to contemplate. "The greatest despotism on earth," says De

Tocqueville, "is an excited, untaught public sentiment; and we should hate not only despots, but despotism. When I feel the hand of power lie heavy on my brow, I care not to know who oppresses me; the yoke is not the easier, because it is held out to me by a million of men."

The danger from this source is intensified by the immense immigration from abroad which is going on, and which bids fair very greatly to increase. The great majority of those who seek our shores, come here ignorant. With little knowledge of any kind, and with no knowledge whatever of the nature of republican institutions, these men, almost at once, are made sharers of the popular sovereignty, with all its tremendous powers of peace and war, order and anarchy, life and death. Not to have a system of public education, by which these ignorant and dangerous masses shall be enlightened, and shall be assimilated to the rest, and to the better part, of the population, is simply suicidal. Our national life hangs upon our common schools.

Besides this grave political consideration, affecting the interests of the entire body politic, and the question of the success and stability of our national institutions, there is another consideration coming home closely and individually to each man's personal interests. Where the law of trial by jury prevails, every citizen, whether educated or ignorant, takes part in the administration of justice. Twelve men, taken indiscriminately from the mass of the people, or if with any discrimination, taken more frequently from the lower walks of life than from the higher, are placed in a jury box to decide upon almost every possible question of human interests. The jury decides your fortune, your reputation. The jury says whether you live or die. Go into a court of justice. Are they light matters which those twelve men are to determine? Look at the anxious faces of those whose estates, whose good name, whose worldly all hangs upon the intelligence of those twelve men, or of any one of them. What assurance have you, save that which comes from popular education, that these men will understand and do their duty? Who would like to trust his legal rights or his personal safety to the verdict of a jury of Neapolitan lazzaroni?

In a few short years, the idle boys who are now prowling about the streets and alleys of our towns, the wharf-rats of our cities, will be a part of our jurymen. Is it of no consequence to me, whether their minds shall be early trained and disciplined, so that they will be capable of following a train of argument, or of comprehending a statement of facts? How is it possible to administer justice with any degree of fairness and efficiency, where the majority of those who are to constitute the jurymen and the witnesses are stolidly ignorant? By common law, every man has a right to be tried by his peers. Let law then provide that those shall, in some substantial sense, be my peers, on whose voice my all in life may depend.

But let us recur once more to the economical part of the argument. When a community is taxed for the support of common schools, the question naturally rises among the taxpayers, Is the system worth the cost? Does the community, by the diffusion of knowledge and education, gain enough to counterbalance the large expense which such education involves? Even if this question could not be answered in the affirmative, it would not follow that common schools should be dispensed with. Common schools are needed as the best and cheapest protection against the crimes incident to an ignorant and degraded population. Common schools are right and proper, because without them the majority of those created in the image of God will never attain to that noble manhood which is their rightful inheritance. But the argument will receive additional force, if it can be shown that general education increases the wealth of the community.

That education does have this effect is evident, I think, from two independent lines of argument. First, an intelligent, educated man is capable individually of achieving greater material results than one who is ignorant. Secondly, the general diffusion of intelligence through a community leads to labor-saving inventions, and thus increases its producing power.

In regard to the first line of argument, some curious and instructive facts were collected a few years since by the late Horace Mann. His inquiries were directed to the efficiency of operatives in factories, a class of men who would seem to require as little general intelligence as any kind of laborers. It was found that, as a general rule, those operatives who could sign their names to their weekly receipts for money, were able to do one-third more work, and to do it better, than those who made their mark. Nor is this at all to be wondered at. There is no kind of work, done by the aid of human muscle, that is purely mechanical. Mind is partner in all that the body does. Mind directs and controls muscle, and even in emergency gives it additional energy and power. No matter how simple the process in which an operative may be engaged, some cultivation of his mental powers is needed. Without it he misdirects his own movements, and mistakes continually the orders of his superintending workman. A boy who has been to a good common school, and has had his mental activities quickened, and whose mind has been stimulated and roused by worthy motives, not only will be more industrious for it when he becomes a man, but his industry will be more effective. He will accomplish more, even as a day laborer, than the mere ignorant boor. When we come to any kind of skilled labor, the difference between the educated and the ignorant is still more apparent. An intelligent mechanic is worth twice as much as one ignorant and stupid.

Many years ago a very instructive fact on this point came under my own personal observation. A gentleman of my acquaintance had frequent need of the aid of a carpenter. The work to be done was not regular carpentry, but various odd jobs, alterations and adaptations to suit special wants, and no little time and materials were wasted in the perpetual misconceptions and mistakes of the successive workmen employed. At length a workman was sent who was a German, from the kingdom of Prussia. After listening attentively to the orders given, and doing what he could to understand what his employer wanted, Michael would whip out his pencil, and in two or three minutes, with a few rapid lines, would present a sketch of the article, so clear that any one could recognize it at a glance. It could be seen at once, also, whether the intention of his employer had been rightly conceived, and whether it was practicable. The consequence was, that so long as Michael was employed, there was no more waste of materials and time, to say nothing of the vexation of continued failures. Michael was not really more skilful as a carpenter than the many others who had preceded him. But his knowledge of drawing, gained in a common school in his native country, made his services worth from fifty cents to a dollar a day more than those of any other workman in the shop, and he actually received two dollars a day, when others in the same shop were receiving only a dollar and a quarter. He was always in demand, and he always received extra wages, and his work even at that rate was considered cheap.

What was true of Michael in carpentry, would be true of any other department of mechanical industry. In cabinet-making, in shoe-making, in tailoring, in masonry, in upholstery, in the various contrivances of tin and sheet iron with which our houses are made comfortable, in gas-fitting and plumbing, in the thousand-and-one necessities of the farm, the garden, and the kitchen, a workman who is ready and expert with his pencil, who has learned to put his own ideas, or those of another, rapidly on paper, is worth fifty per cent. more than his fellows who have not this skill.

The example of this man was brought vividly to my mind at a later day, in Philadelphia, when an important educational question was under discussion. Rembrandt Peale had two dreams, each worthy of his genius.

One was to paint a Washington which should go down to posterity; the other was so to simplify the elements of the art of drawing that young boys and girls might learn it as universally as they learn to read and write. He spent long years in maturing a little work for this purpose, no bigger than a primer or a spelling-book, and a determined effort was made on the part of some of the friends of popular education to introduce the study into the primary public schools of Philadelphia. It was introduced into the High Schools. But its benefits were limited to a comparatively small number. The hope and the aim of the friends of Mr. Peale's project were to make the study an elementary one—to make a certain amount of proficiency in drawing a test of promotion from the lower schools to the schools above it. This would have placed "Graphics" alongside of the copy-book and the spelling-book. After struggling for several years with popular prejudice, the friends of the scheme were obliged to abandon it as hopeless. The idea was too much in advance of the times. Could the plan have succeeded, and could the entire youthful population of that great city, which is preëminently a mechanical and manufacturing centre, have grown up with a familiar practised skill in the use of the pencil, in ordinary, off-hand drawing, such as our friend Michael had, there can be no question that it would have added untold millions to the general wealth. If every boy and girl in that great metropolitan city were now obliged to spend as much time in learning to draw as is spent in learning to spell, and at the same age that they learn to spell, I do soberly believe that the addition to the wealth of the city, by the increased mechanical skill that would be developed, would be worth more than the entire cost of her public schools, although they do cost well-nigh a million of dollars annually.

What is true of drawing, is true of every branch and accomplishment necessary to a complete education. A man is educated when all his capacities bodily and mental are developed, and a community is educated when all its members are. Now if we could imagine two communities, of exactly equal numbers, and in physical circumstances exactly equal as to climate, soil, access to markets, and so forth, and if one of these communities should tax itself to the extent of even one-fourth of its income in promoting popular education, while the other spent not a dollar in this way, there can be little doubt as to which community would make the most rapid advances in wealth and in every other desirable social good.

We happen to have on this subject one most striking and significant record. In 1670, the English Commissioners for Foreign Plantations addressed to the Governors of the several colonies a series of questions concerning the condition of the settlements under their charge. One of these questions related to the means of popular education. The answers of two of the Governors are preserved. One of them, the Governor of Connecticut, ruled a territory to which nature had not been specially propitious. Its climate was bleak, its coast rockbound, its soil blest with only ordinary fertility. The other territory, Virginia, had an extraordinary amount of natural advantages. It had fine harbors, numerous navigable streams, a climate more temperate by several degrees than its rival, the soil in its lowlands and valleys unsurpassed in any of the Plantations for its capacity to produce wheat, corn, and tobacco, its mountains filled with untold treasures of lime, iron, and coal, (and, it now seems, with petroleum also,) and withal that wonderful variety of natural resources, which seems best suited to stimulate and reward the productive industry of its inhabitants.

The Governor of the less favored colony replied to the Royal Commissioners, as follows: "*One-fourth* of the annual revenue of the Colony is laid out in maintaining free schools for the education of our children." The policy thus early impressed upon the colony has been maintained with steadfast and almost proverbial consistency to this day, that region being known the world over as the land of schoolmasters. The Governor of the other colony replied, "I thank God, there are no free schools, nor printing, and I hope we shall not have, these hundred years." To this policy she also has until lately only too faithfully adhered. Now what is the result?

By referring to the tables accompanying the Census of 1860, we find the following significant facts.

1. The average cash value of land was not quite $12 an acre in one commonwealth (Virginia), and a little over $36 an acre in the other.

2. One commonwealth sustained only five inhabitants to every hundred acres of her soil, the other sustained eighteen inhabitants to every hundred acres.

3. The value of all property, real and personal, aver-

aged by the population, was in one commonwealth $496 to every inhabitant, in the other $965 to every inhabitant.

4. The value of all property, real and personal, averaged by the acre, was in one commonwealth less than $26 to the acre, in the other more than $177 to the acre.

To which facts I may add, what is true, though not in the Census, it was the invention of Eli Whitney, a travelling schoolmaster from Connecticut, that has trebled the value of land in nearly every Southern State.

I have been endeavoring to show that popular education, though it is expensive, tends to national wealth. The argument is that an educated population is capable of producing greater material results than a population uneducated can produce. The example of Eli Whitney, just referred to, suggests the other line of argument, which I shall now notice briefly in conclusion. This second argument is, that the general diffusion of intelligence in a community tends to quicken invention, and leads to the discovery of those scientific principles and of those ingenious labor-saving machines, by which the productive power of the community is so greatly multiplied. The cotton-gin, the steam-engine, the sewing-machine, and the reaping-machine would never have been invented in a nation of boors. It is not asserted that every boy who goes to school will become an inventor. But it is as certain as the laws of mind and matter can make it, that inventions abound in a nation in proportion to its progress in science and the general spread of intelligence among the masses. Multiply common schools and you multiply inventions. How much these latter increase man's producing power, and so add to the aggregate of human wealth, it is needless to say. The invention of Watt alone has quadrupled the productive power of the whole human race. The aggregate steam-power of one single country, Great Britain, equals the muscular capacity for labor of four hundred millions of men—more than twice the number of adult males capable of labor on our planet. Its aggregate power throughout the earth is equal to the male capacity for manual work of four or five worlds like ours. The commerce, the navigation, the maritime warfare, the agriculture, the mechanic arts of the human race, have been revolutionized by this single invention not yet a century old.

The application of scientific truths to the common industries of life is becoming every day more and more a necessity. The village carpenter, no less than the builder of the Niagara Suspension Bridge, makes hourly reference to scientific laws. The carpenter who misapplies his formulæ for the strength of materials, builds a house which falls down. The properties of the various mechanical powers are involved in every machine. Every machine, indeed, it has been well said, is a solidified mechanical theorem. The surveyor in determining the limits of one's farm, the architect in planning a house, the builder in planning his estimates, and the several master workmen who do the carpentry, masonry, and finishing, are all dependent upon geometric truths. Bleaching, dyeing, calico-printing, gas-making, soap-making, sugar-refining, the reduction of metals from their ores, with innumerable other productive industries, are dependent upon chemistry.

Agriculture, the basis of all the other arts, is in the same condition. Chemical knowledge, indeed, is doing for the productive powers of the soil what the application of steam has done for the increase of mechanical power. The farmer who wishes to double his crops, finds the means of doing so, not in multiplying his acres, but in applying a knowledge of the laws of chemistry to the cultivation of the soil already possessed. Even physiology is adding to the wealth of the farming interest. The truth that the production of animal heat implies waste of substance, and that therefore preventing the loss of heat prevents the need for extra food—which is a purely theoretical conclusion—now guides the fattening of cattle. By keeping cattle warm, fodder is saved. Experiments of physiologists have proved, not only that change of diet is beneficial, but that digestion is facilitated by a mixture of ingredients in each meal. Both these truths are now influencing cattle-feeding. In the keen race of competition, the farmer who has a competent knowledge of the laws of animal and vegetable physiology and of agricultural chemistry, will surely distance the one who gropes along by guess and by tradition. A general diffusion of scientific knowledge saves the community from innumerable wasteful and foolish mistakes. In England, not many years ago, the partners in a large mining company were ruined from not knowing that a certain fossil belonged to the old red sandstone, below which coal is never found. In another enterprise, £20,000 were lost in the prosecution of a scheme for collecting the alcohol that distils from bread in baking, all of which might have been saved, had the parties known that less than one hundredth part by weight of the flour is changed in fermentation.

But it is not necessary to multiply illustrations. Suffice it to say, in conclusion, I hold it to be a most manifest truth, that the general education of a community increases largely its material wealth, both by the direct effect which knowledge has upon individuals in making them individually more productive, and by the increased control which the diffusion of knowledge gives to mankind over the powers of nature. A nation or a state is wisely economical which spends largely and even lavishly upon popular education.

XXX.

WHAT IS EDUCATION?

MY last chapter, like the first, begins with a question. Strange to say, no satisfactory definition of education has yet been given, nor has a definition of it often been even attempted. The literature of the subject is copious enough. But writers have busied themselves mainly with details, with methods of teaching, and so forth. A few, of a more philosophical turn of mind, have discussed the principles of the subject, and among these some have undertaken to develop their theories from the true starting-point of a definition. But among all these, from Plato, who was the earliest systematic writer on the subject, to Herbert Spencer, the latest and the most pretentious, not one has given a definition of it which is not open to objection.

It may seem presumptuous, perhaps, to undertake again that in which so many have failed. But there can be no harm in making at least an endeavor. What then are some of the elements which enter into our idea of education?

To educate is, in the first place, to develop. It is to draw out and strengthen the powers and give them right direction. It is, therefore, something more than merely imparting knowledge. Knowledge is to the child's mind what food is to the body. Each is a means to an end. It is to cause growth. As by the proper use of food and exercise the limbs and muscles expand, and acquire their full and appointed size, symmetry, and strength, so by acquiring and using knowledge of various kinds, the various faculties of the mind attain their full power and proportion. For this reason mainly the pure mathematics and the ancient languages, Latin and Greek, have held their place in almost every course of liberal study, not because the knowledge of these branches is likely to be called for in ordinary professional business, but because the study of these branches is supposed to be particularly adapted to develop and invigorate certain important qualities of the mind. This development of the powers, then, is the first element involved in a just idea of education.

But, secondly, nature plainly indicates a certain order to be observed in the development of the faculties. "First the blade, then the ear, after that the full corn in the ear." So in the human plant. The time for the efflorescence of some of the faculties is in early youth. Other faculties make little growth till near the age of manhood. A wise educator will carefully observe these facts, and not waste his energies and mar his work, either by attempting a premature development of those faculties which God seems to have meant to ripen later, or by neglecting to draw out and train in childhood those faculties which then most naturally and aptly spring into vigorous growth. Youth, for instance, is the season, of all others, when the memory is to be cultivated; the season of all others, when the instinctive principle of faith is to have free play. So, too, the moral and emotional faculties may receive the first germs of their development at a very early stage in the history of the human being. The education of this part of our nature begins, indeed, with the first smile of recognition that passes between the infant and its mother. Other faculties and powers, as the reason and the judgment, for instance, come to maturity nearer the age of manhood, and the normal period for their cultivation is accordingly near the end, rather than near the beginning, of an educational course. It is not, however, my object here to mark out an order for the development of the faculties, but only to note that there is such an order, and that the observance of this order is a most important element in our idea of what education is.

The next element in this idea is that a certain proportion and symmetry be observed in the development of the powers. Perhaps it might not be strictly accurate to say that any faculty may be cultivated too highly. Yet there certainly is an excess whenever one faculty or power is cultivated quite out of proportion to the other faculties and powers. A man in Boston a few years ago, by directing his attention exclusively for a long time to the single act of lifting, educated his body to the power of lifting enormous weights. But this power was gained at the expense of agility, grace, and many other bodily qualities quite as important as that of lifting weights. So the mental faculties may become one-sided by injudicious training. The memory may be inordinately developed at the expense of the reasoning power, the reason at the expense of the imagination, the feelings at the expense of the judgment, the mind at the expense of the body, the body at the expense of the mind. In all right education, therefore, the faculties are to be developed, not only in due order, but in due proportion.

The next element that enters into our idea is that of a proper comprehensiveness. The educator must bear in mind that the being committed to his care is one of a complex nature, and that every part of this complex nature is to receive its due attention. Physical education is included in his duties as well as mental, mental as well as moral and religious. No part is to be neglected. He should aim to secure for his subject full bodily health, agility, strength, symmetry, and power of endurance. The bodily senses are capable of a degree of cultivation that few seem to be aware of. Perhaps, in our ordinary schemes of education, no part of our complex nature is so inadequately provided for, so almost ignored, as the physical. But, as in regard to the other points that have been raised, so here, it is not my object so much to particularize the several parts of human nature that require attention, as to recognize distinctly the fact that we are thus complex, and that the business of the educator is necessarily a many-sided one, requiring most varied knowledge and experience.

But there is one important limitation to be observed here, otherwise our definition would be seriously amiss. In many works on education, it is stated, without qualification, that we ought to give to all our powers the fullest development of which they are capable. If we were unfallen angels, the rule might perhaps be a safe one. But for fallen human beings, it certainly needs some limitation. We have faculties and powers, not a few, which we need to repress rather than to cultivate. Are we to give the fullest development of which they are capable, to anger, envy, jealousy, cunning, avarice, and lust? To state the question is to answer it. It is not every faculty of the child, therefore, that is to be developed, but only those parts of his nature which are good and desirable, those by which he can best discharge his duties to God and attain his highest excellence as a man.

Let us now gather up the several ideas which have been suggested, and see if we cannot compress them into some brief formula, as a definition of education, which, if not perfect and exhaustive of the subject, shall be both more comprehensive and more precise than those now afloat.

Definition.—Education is developing, in due order and proportion, whatever is good and desirable in human nature.

Model Text Books

FOR

SCHOOLS, ACADEMIES AND COLLEGES.

A NEW EDITION OF THE CLASSICS.

CHASE & STUART'S CLASSICAL SERIES.

EDITED BY

THOMAS CHASE, A.M., PROFESSOR OF CLASSICAL LITERATURE, *Haverford College*, Penna.

&

GEORGE STUART, A.M., PROFESSOR OF THE LATIN LANGUAGE, *Central High School*, Philada.

REFERENCES TO

HARKNESS'S LATIN GRAMMAR,

AND

ANDREWS & STODDARD'S LATIN GRAMMAR.

THE publication of this edition of the Classics was suggested by the constantly increasing demand by teachers for an edition which, by judicious notes, would give to the student the assistance really necessary to render his study profitable, furnishing explanations of passages difficult of interpretation, of peculiarities of syntax, &c., and yet would require him to make faithful use of his grammar and dictionary.

It is believed that this Classical Series needs only to be known to insure its very general use. The publishers claim for it peculiar merit, and beg leave to call attention to the following important particulars:

The purity of the texts.

The clearness and conciseness of the notes, and their adaptation to the wants of students.

The beauty of the type and paper.

The handsome style of binding.

The convenience of the shape and size.

The low price at which the volumes are sold.

The preparation of the whole Series is the *original work* of American scholars.

The texts are not *mere reprints*, but are based upon a careful and painstaking comparison of *all the most improved editions*, with constant reference to the authority of the best manuscripts.

No pains have been spared to make the notes accurate, clear, and *helpful to the learner.* Points of geography, history, mythology, and antiquities are explained in accordance with the views of the best German scholars. The references to the grammars most in use in this country, viz.:

HARKNESS'S LATIN GRAMMAR

AND

ANDREWS & STODDARD'S LATIN GRAMMAR,

is in itself an advantage to be gained only by the use of this edition.

Desirous of affording Professors and Teachers of Latin throughout the entire country an opportunity of becoming acquainted with these books, the publishers will send copies for examination, gratis, to every Teacher of Latin in the United States, on application, accompanied by a catalogue of the institution with which he is connected, or of which he is the Principal.

The Series, when complete, will consist of

CÆSAR'S COMMENTARIES,
VIRGIL'S ÆNEID,
CICERO'S ORATIONS,
HORACE, SALLUST and LIVY,

Of which there are now ready the following, viz.:

CÆSAR'S COMMENTARIES on the Gallic War. With Explanatory Notes, a Vocabulary, Geographical Index, Map of Gaul, Plan of the Bridge, &c., &c. By Prof. GEORGE STUART. Price by mail, postpaid, $1.25. Per dozen, by express, $11.25.

The text of Cæsar has been carefully compared with that of Kraner, Oehler, Nepperdey, and other distinguished editors. Much care has been bestowed upon this portion of the work, and it is hoped that whatever improvements have been introduced into the text by the learning and research of the German editors named, will be found in the present edition.

The Notes have been prepared with a very simple view,—to give the student that amount and kind of assistance which are really necessary to render his study profitable; to remove difficulties greater than his strength ; and to afford or direct him to the sources of such information as is requisite to a thorough understanding of the author.

VIRGIL'S ÆNEID. With Explanatory Notes, Metrical Index, Remarks on Classical Versification, Index of Proper Names, &c. By Prof. THOMAS CHASE. Price by mail, postpaid, $1.50. Per dozen, by express, $13.50.

The text of the Æneid here presented is based upon a careful collation of the editions of Heyne, Wagner, Conington, Ladewig, and Ribbeck, with frequent reference to other standard authorities, and with constant and especial regard to the testimony of the best manuscripts. In the preparation of the Notes, the endeavor has been made to meet the actual wants of students in our schools. Frequent references are made to the grammars most in use, and explanations are furnished of passages difficult of interpretation, of peculiarities of syntax, and of such points of history, geography, mythology, and antiquities, as require elucidation. A metrical index has been added, in which the chief difficulties of scanning are solved. One thing is presumed throughout,—that the student will make a faithful use of his grammar and dictionary, the only way in which true scholars are made.

CICERO and HORACE will be issued about Dec. 1868.
SALLUST and LIVY, during the following year.

The unprecedented demand for the first two volumes of this Series during the past few months evidences their adaptation to the actual wants of the recitation room. Testimonials have been received from a large number of the most flourishing classical institutions of the country, in which they have already been adopted as text-books, and the Principals of hundreds of schools have expressed their intention to commence their next term with these standard works. From every source but a single opinion has been expressed, viz.: that the publishers have more than fulfilled their promise in presenting a series of books which will be eagerly sought after by every student of the classics.

A MANUAL OF ELOCUTION. Founded upon the Philosophy of the Human Voice, with Classified Illustrations, Suggested by and Arranged to meet the Practical Difficulties of Instruction. By M. S. MITCHELL. Price by mail, postpaid, $1.50. Per dozen, by express, $13.50.

The compiler cannot conceal the hope that this glimpse of our general literature may tempt to individual research among its treasures, so varied and inexhaustible;—that this text-book for the school-room may become not only teacher, but friend, to those in whose hands it is placed, and while aiding, through systematic development and training of the elocutionary powers of the pupil, to overcome many of the practical difficulties of instruction, may accomplish a higher work in the cultivation and refinement of character.

To afford teachers an idea of the character of the work, we append a list of the

SUBJECTS TREATED OF.

Articulation, Pronunciation, Accent, Emphasis, Modulation, Melody of Speech, Pitch, Tone, Inflections, Sense, Cadence, Force, Stress, Grammatical and Rhetorical Pauses, Movement, Reading of Poetry, Faults in the Reading of Poetry, Action, Attitude, Analysis of the Principles of Gestures, and Oratory.

Among the *gems of literature* collected in this volume may be named the following, which will give a general idea of the character of the selections for practice, of which the volume is largely composed.

A Psalm of Life.
Address at Gettysburg.
Barbara Frietchie.
Bonny Kelmeny.
Bugle Song.
Charge of the Light Brigade.
Death of Little Nell.
Dies Iræ.
Elegy in a Country Churchyard.
Excelsior.
Godiva.
Invocation to Light.
Laus Deo.
The American Flag.
Oh! why should the Spirit of Mortal be Proud?
The Battle of Ivry.
The Bells.
The Bridge of Sighs.
The Great Bell Roland.
The Mantle of St. John de Matha.
The Raven.
The Soldier from Bingen.
The Song of the Shirt.
Union and Liberty.
Woman's Education.
Work.

THE MODEL DEFINER, with Sentences showing the Proper Use of Words. An Elementary Work, containing Definitions and Etymology for the Little Ones. By A. C. WEBB. Price by mail, postpaid, 25 cents. Per dozen, by express, $2.16.

THE MODEL ETYMOLOGY. Giving not only the Definitions, Etymology, and Analysis, but that which can be obtained only from an intimate acquaintance with the best Authors, viz.: **The Correct Use of Words.** By A. C. WEBB. Price by mail, postpaid, 60 cents. Per dozen, by express, $5.40.

The importance of words cannot be over-estimated. Knowledge can be imparted and received only by the medium of words, correctly used and properly understood. The basis of a good education must be laid with words, well chosen, properly arranged, and firmly implanted in the mind. From the richness of the English Language, which gives many words to the same meaning, and many and diverse meanings to the same word, the proper *use* of a word cannot be deduced from its *meaning*. How, then, is the knowledge of the use of words to be imparted to children? Either by the teacher, or by conversation and reading. By the latter method the knowledge acquired is limited in extent; and as it is entirely dependent on the power of observation, the impressions received are faint and ill-defined, and the conclusions arrived at, frequently incorrect. The practice of Arithmetic might possibly be left to such teaching, inasmuch as Arithmetic is an exact science based on fixed principles, from which correct *reasoning* must deduce correct *results*. But no reasoning can show to the child who has learned "*Deduce, to draw*," that he must not say, "I tried *to deduce* the horse from the stable;" or, "*Deciduous, falling*." "The boy, *deciduous* from the window, was killed." The importance and difficulty of the work demands that it shall not be left to the uncertainties of home teaching. The labor involved forbids that this essential part of education shall be imposed on the parent. Like Arithmetic, or any other department of knowledge, it should be performed by the teacher, in the time specially set apart for mental training. The plan adopted in the **Model Word-Book Series** is not new. All good Dictionaries illustrate the meaning by a Model. To quote from a *good author*, a sentence containing the word, as proof of its correct use, is the only authority allowed. A simple trial of the work either by requiring the child to form sentences similar to those given, or by memorizing the sentences as models for future use, will convince any one of the following advantages to be derived from the Model Word-Book Series:

1. Saving of Time.
2. Increased Knowledge of Words.
3. Ease to Teacher and Scholar.
4. A Knowledge of the Correct Use of Words.

THE YOUNG STUDENT'S COMPANION; or, Elementary Lessons and Exercises in Translating from English into French. By M. A. LONGSTRETH, Principal of a Seminary for Young Ladies, Philadelphia. Price by mail, postpaid, $1.00. Per dozen, by express, $9.00.

The object of this little work is to present to the young student a condensed view of the elements of the French language, in a clear and simple manner, and, at the same time, to lessen the fatigue incurred by the teacher in giving repeated verbal explanations of the most important rules of etymology. No attempt has been made to teach the syntax of the language, with the exception of a few fundamental rules; neither have many idioms been introduced; the aim of the compiler being to avoid whatever might perplex or confuse.

This little work, it will be remembered, is not intended to take the place of a Grammar, but to prepare the pupil, by careful drilling, for larger and more comprehensive treatises; and it is believed that any child, who can distinguish the different parts of speech in English, will be able to understand and learn the lessons without difficulty; and that, if they are thoroughly learned, the succeeding course of French study will be much facilitated. In its preparation, the best authorities have been carefully consulted and followed, and assistance has been kindly furnished by several Professors of the French language, whose experience in teaching enables them to judge of the wants of the young student.

MARTINDALE'S HISTORY OF THE UNITED STATES. From the Discovery of America to the close of the late Rebellion. By JOSEPH C. MARTINDALE, M.D., Principal of the Madison Grammar School, Philadelphia. Price by mail, postpaid, 60 cents. Per dozen, by express, $5.40.

The want of a History suitable for the Schoolroom has long been felt by educators. In most instances, the Histories presented have been too much encumbered with details of but little service to the pupils. This has been one of the causes which has prevented History from being one of the usual branches of study in our Common Schools outside of cities and towns; none can so well appreciate the difficulties which have surrounded this subject as the teacher. Another cause which has precluded the study of History has been the high price of all the text-books on this subject. The very low price of the present treatise will obviate this difficulty. The author of this compend, a man of large experience in the schoolroom, deserves the thanks of teachers and scholars, for the concise and succinct form in which he has treated this much neglected subject; ignoring all that does not properly appertain to the important events of our Nation's existence, he has given us all that should be memorized, and in so agreeable a form as to be thoroughly mastered with but little effort.

With this book in his hand, the scholar can in a single school-term obtain as complete a knowledge of the History of the United States as has heretofore required double the time and effort.

Teachers who are anxious to have their pupils proficient in this subject, or who are themselves desirous of reviewing the main points of History in order to pass a creditable examination, will find this *the book for their purposes*, and it will commend itself to the *live teacher as a book long needed*. The want of such a work suggested its preparation, and we are satisfied that in every schoolroom its advent will be welcomed by both teacher and pupil.

The unprecedented success which has attended this work since its publication is the best recommendation of its merits, more than *Twenty Thousand Copies* having been sold during the past year. It is indorsed by prominent educators, is used in over fifty Normal Schools, and in hundreds of cities, towns, and townships throughout the entire country. Teachers, Directors, and all others interested in Elementary Education are invited to examine the book.

PARKER'S GRAMMAR OF THE ENGLISH LANGUAGE. Based upon an Analysis of the English Sentence. With copious Examples and Exercises in Parsing and the Correction of False Syntax, and an Appendix, containing Critical and Explanatory Notes, and Lists of Peculiar and Exceptional Forms. For the use of Schools and Academies, and those who write. By WM. HENRY PARKER, Principal of Ringgold Grammar School, Philadelphia. Price by mail, postpaid, $1.25.

Prepared by a GRAMMAR SCHOOL PRINCIPAL, and arranged in the manner that many years of research and actual experience in the schoolroom have demonstrated to be the best for teaching, this book commends itself to teachers as a simple, progressive, and consistent treatise on Grammar, the need of which has so long been recognized. We ask for it a careful and critical examination. The thorough acquaintance of the author with his subject, and his practical knowledge of the difficulties which beset the teacher in the use of the text-book, and the necessity for the teacher's supplying deficiencies and omissions and amending the text to suit constructions found daily in parsing, and in other practical exercises in Grammar, have enabled him to prepare a work which will, on trial, be found a labor-saving aid to both teacher and pupil.

THE MODEL POCKET REGISTER AND GRADE-BOOK. A Roll-Book. Register and Record combined.

Adapted to any grade of School, from Primary to College. Handsomely and durably bound in fine Cloth. Price by mail, postpaid, 65 cents. Per dozen, by express, $6.00.

Prof. E. A. Sheldon, of the New York State Normal School, and author of "Lessons on Objects," and "Elementary Instruction," says of this book:

"Your Model Pocket Register is just the thing every teacher needs. I shall never again be without one."

THE MODEL SCHOOL-DIARY.

Designed as an aid in securing the co-operation of parents. It consists of a Record of the Attendance, Deportment, Recitations, &c., of a Scholar, for every day in the week. At the close of the week it is to be sent to the parent or guardian, for his examination and signature. Teachers will find in this Diary an article that has long been needed. Its low cost will insure its general use. Copies will be mailed to teachers for examination, postpaid, on receipt of ten cents. Price per dozen, by mail, postpaid, $1.00. Per dozen, by express, 84 cents.

REWARDS OF MERIT.

As there are many teachers who make use of these incentives to study, we have endeavored to meet the demand, with what success the teacher can judge after seeing our specimens. They are printed on the best quality of Bristol card, colored in gold, silver, crimson, ultra-marine, and emerald, and are executed in the highest style of the lithographic art. They are chaste, ornate, and beautiful, and need but be seen to be appreciated. The teacher will, of course, not connect these gems of art with the common colored cards in vogue. Price per set by mail, postpaid, 35 cents.

Please address the Publishers,

ELDREDGE & BROTHER,

17 & 19 South Sixth Street,

PHILADELPHIA, PA.

www.ingramcontent.com/pod-product-compliance
Lightning Source LLC
LaVergne TN
LVHW010219110826
845151LV00004B/1139

* 9 7 8 1 4 2 5 5 2 6 1 9 1 *